How to Keep Your Woman

— *And Keep Her the Way You Love Her*

How to Keep Your Woman

— *And Keep Her the Way You Love Her*

Linda Nilson, Ph.D.

Emerald Wing Press LLC
Seneca, SC

How to Keep Your Woman – And Keep Her the Way You Love Her

Copyright © by Linda Nilson 2010

All rights reserved.

Front cover photograph by Kris Bauernfeind

Graphics assistance provided by Kathy Kegley and Jan Lay

No part of this book may be reproduced or transmitted in any form or by any means, electronic or mechanical, including photocopying, recording, or by any information storage or retrieval system, without permission in writing from the publisher or the author.

ISBN-13   978-0-9841657-8-0

ISBN-10   0-9841657-8-9

Emerald Wing Press LLC
Seneca, SC

Printed in the United States of America

Contents

Preface   ix

1. Why Keeping Your Woman Is a Problem   1
2. Why Keeping Your Woman Is *Your* Responsibility   14
3. Viva la Difference and End the Battle of the Sexes   28
4. Keeping Her vs. Keeping Her the Way You Love Her: What Do You Want to Keep in Your Woman?   47
5. How to Tell She's Going to Seed – Before It's Too Late   54
6. How to Tell She's Going – Before You Lose Her   69
7. What a Man *Thinks* Has Happened When He Loses His Woman   75
8. What's *Really* Happening: How a Man Loses His Woman   81
9. How a Man Can Keep Her – and Keep Her the Way He Loves Her   91
10. Common Pitfalls and How to Avoid Them   103
11. Special Cases: Women Who Are Harder to Keep   136
12. How to Get Her Back – Maybe   152
13. When to Let Go   157
14. Is It Worth the Effort?   168

To all the men I've loved before

Preface

I didn't know how much a woman could mean to a man until a dear graduate school friend of mine – brilliant, perceptive, destined to be a scholarly superstar – flunked his qualifying exams. It didn't make any sense to me. I figured some pompous professor had it in for Jeff. So I dropped by the married student housing barracks to find out whodunit to him and to steady his confidence.

It took several knocks. He barely glanced a "hi" as he let me in. The place was a mess – stacks of dirty laundry where the couch had been, nails on the wall where pictures had hung, and empty stacks of bricks and boards. The exams slipped my mind.

"Where's Meg?" I asked as innocently as I could fake.

"Gone. She left me just before exams."

"But – why?" The telling scene hadn't cushioned the shock. He dropped into the remaining chair and studied the knee patch on his jeans.

"I don't know . . . I just don't know."

And he had thought about nothing else for weeks, including his exams. He thought about a little else for a long time afterwards. But he never quite got his mind around it. Or his heart over it.

I didn't know Meg all that well, but I *am* a *woman*. *I did* know why she left, though I found her timing tacky.

Jeff was warm, trustworthy, loyal, and infinitely likeable. A prince of a man. It's just that he never quite understood Meg's increasing sense of loneliness, of Paradise Lost, and her frustration trying to find it with him again.

Maybe I should have said something to him. I was worried that he might come up empty-bedded again (he did). But I was so taken aback by his utter disintegration. He seemed like a man too weak for the operation that might save his life. Yet he hadn't impressed me before as any more or less emotional than the next guy. Besides, I wasn't in the best place to fully empathize. I myself had just gotten beyond believing that men got married so they could stop thinking about sex and get some work done.

Since then, I've seen this romantic tragedy replayed again and again: Boy gets girl. Boy loses girl, and doesn't know why. Boy falls apart. And I'm genuinely concerned. I *really* like you men. I like the pleasure of your company, whatever the pleasure. You make great friends. You're true brothers. I've even fallen in love with several of you. So I hate to see any of you suffer. You're well intended and really want to make your woman happy. It's sad that women misconstrue the intentions behind so many of the things you do. Their needs don't express themselves the same way yours do either.

Of course, *only a woman* can tell you the woman's interpretation. And your woman may be too tongue-tied by her own head trips to translate for herself. So it's about time that some other woman do it for her, *for you*. I care enough to try, and I owe it to Jeff.

Keeping your woman, and keeping her the woman you love, is all such a heavy subject that it could get morosely melodramatic and sickly psychiatric. So I'm going to lighten it up a bit without making light of it. You don't mind a little teasing, do you? A chance to smile at yourself and your woman? Some tenderly intended tough talk? And you *do* want to see how your world looks through your woman's eyes, even when she gives you an irreverent wink, right? Wonderful. Then let me share with you some womanly wisdom about women.

But who am *I* to advise *you*? You have a right to ask. Here I am prying into your most private, primary affairs and telling you how to run them better. Why should *you* listen to *me*?

Well, let's start with my most impressive, but not necessarily most important, credentials. I earned my Ph.D. in sociology roughly from the best program in the nation at the time (the University of Wisconsin, Madison), or so the ratings said. Since then I've taught, done research, and published in the field. I know my way around the professional books and journals in sociology, psychology, and counseling as well as I know my own kitchen. And I've read the latest findings on male-female relationships, their differences, their problems, family dynamics, and life changes. All kinds of studies have been done, and most of them are credibly scientific and incredibly interesting. It's just too bad that so few people know about them. Of course, they're written in so much psycho-technical jargon and sprinkled with so many mathematical machinations that you can't decipher them without advanced degrees in either social science or code-cracking. And few scholarly types bother to descend their Ivory

Tower to tell the world their latest scoop. But I happen to enjoy it as I find the air can be rather thin and cold way up there in the clouds. Usable knowledge ought to be made useful and be used, right?

As a sociologist, I take the view that White Knights and Fair Ladies, as well as Bastards and Bitches, are *made*, not born. So they can be *re*made, too. If you treat a person like he or she is charming, smart, and sexy, he or she will become at least a little more like that. People respond well to others having a positive image of them; they start to reflect that image like a mirror. They rise to the occasion, at least as far as biology and experience can take them. Of course, it works in the other direction, too. People can sink as low as they're treated. If you expect nothing much from them, that's about as much as you'll get. So the general idea is to build and nurture the best in loved ones – even put them on a short pedestal – and you're likely to get a much better approximation to your ideal than you would otherwise.

Love remakes lovers like that in its early stages. You love a woman because she makes you feel like you're better than you *thought* you were, and you start to *become* that. And vice versa for her. Over time, though, a few let-downs can bum out lovers enough to set the process in reverse. It's a damn shame, because it usually makes matters worse. Lovers can make each other *feel* like less than they are, and *become* that way. Then maybe down the line, one of them meets someone new who makes him or her feel and act like a million bucks again. And poof with the old relationship.

No, love is no place for the fainthearted and easily discouraged. You've got to keep the faith. You've got to *manufacture* it when your inventory is low, because prophesies have a way of fulfilling themselves.

Something I am *not* by profession is a therapist, which some of you may consider a positive credential. I'm not *against* seeking professional help. Under some circumstances, I recommend it. I went through a year of marriage counseling myself and learned a lot about what it does and doesn't offer.

What it *doesn't* do is make one partner who wants out of a relationship turn around and make it better. Nor does it inspire a "lazy" one to work harder at it. What it *can* do is help an *uncertain* partner decide whether he or she *wants* the relationship, and how much.

If both *really* want it, then counseling can teach you what I like to call "good psychological hygiene." It can give you valuable techniques and tricks to tame your temper, flush out conflicts, soften suspicions, and the like. But they don't defy good common sense or the logic of love. And they're not like some pill that magically cures you while you're asleep. *You* have to actively *apply* them between appointments. The *real* work is *home*work. If you're not committed to "solving the problem," these techniques won't work because *you* won't. So you might as well save your money for the divorce. However, if you *are* committed, you might be able to learn them from a book, possibly this one, and blow your bucks on a second and third honeymoon.

But back to who I am to advise you. I'd say my best credential is that I'm a woman. A woman who, being one, innately *understands* women. A woman who has learned (in blushing detail) the love lives and longings of many other women. A woman who has worked with, lived with, and loved a considerable number of men, some who have kept me very happily for years, and others who lost me without meaning to. A woman who, as part of a commuter couple for ten years, had the chance to room and board with a variety of other couples and to eyewitness much of their intimate interaction. A woman who, fortunately, has a knack to get almost anyone to talk about their most private matters.

I'm a "liberated" woman too – a "feminist." Of course, there are as many different versions of "liberation" as there are women. Mine means that I take responsibility for my own livelihood, life style, and love affairs. I don't depend on men for money, values, viewpoints, or my happiness any more than I do on friends. So I maintain control of my own destiny. I've found it much easier and more rewarding to deal with men this way.

In fact, the women I hear crying most bitterly about what bastards and bums you guys are turn out to be the *least liberated*. They trust and lean on you *too* much. They give you all the power and don't look out for themselves. I've observed that the women you "use" the most blatantly *let* themselves get used. They give, give, give for so little in return, while you grow contemptuous of them and take, take, take. Morally speaking, you know you shouldn't do that, but from a power perspective, you're acting as rational as a capitalist.

Why pay a worker who'll work for free? The trouble is, you can't really *respect* her.

Then there are the women you lead on, like the ever-suffering singles who attach themselves to you married men while you're deciding to stay with your wife after all. You're not really the self-seeking scoundrels they say you are; you rarely mislead a woman unless you mislead yourself first. And yes, many of you do pull the wool over your own eyes and, thus, get some pretty fuzzy notions.

So for me, being liberated may mean taking a man's poetry and promises with a sprinkling of skepticism and holding back a bit of my own. It expects honor and intimacy, but allows for changes of heart and circumstance. It may breed restraint amid the romance, but it avoids the traditional lover's traps and keeps both him and me on our toes. After all, a lopsided love is too burdensome to carry; a sudden bonfire runs out of fuel; and a stone-carved commitment either cracks or wears down as the weather changes.

With this brand of liberation, and some luck, I've enjoyed very positive experiences with you men, from my father on up (and he kept his woman for 63 years). You've made as close and trusted friends as women have. Oh, I get plenty pissed with the sexist chauvinists who've refused me my professional due or who've tried to impose their paternalistic opinions on me. (The former get a fight; the latter, flight.) But I've found most of you to be quite reasonable, refreshingly open, and self-critically secure with yourselves, as long as you're getting the love and space to *be* yourself.

So I'm speaking to you not only as a woman who knows and cares about women, but also as a friend who knows and appreciates *you*. And as a friend, I get upset when so many of you unwittingly let your Dearest Delight slip away. I don't think I'm inflating your woman's worth to you either. When I decided to write a book *to* and *for* men, I asked a sensitive, street-wise man, "What do men most want to know that a woman can tell them?" After a pause to ponder, he replied, "How to keep their woman, because their woman is so central to their egos and identity and yet so baffling to keep happy!" There it was, straight from a stallion's mouth.

So I started placing together some sociology and psychology with my friends' and my own experiences, expanding the picture with dozens of heavy interviews with men and women of all ages, educational levels, and marital statuses, and from all walks of life. I talked with "keepers" and "happily kept," "losers" and "lost." And, although the women varied from gung-ho professionals to sturdy blue-collar workers to happy and not-so-happy housewives, it was amazing how similar their desires and disappointments were, as well as their sources of contentment and complaints.

Those in the process of "going" – either out the door or to seed – provided the best data. The door-watchers could say exactly what stage of being lost they were in. They even knew which one they'd come out of and what was up next if their man didn't act fast. And they'd go on and on (and on) about what he had and hadn't done to push them here. Naturally they were angry, but more at having been pushed there than at their man; they all really wanted to be kept.

The seeders – well, of course, they weren't eager to discuss their stage of deterioration. But then they didn't have to; it was obvious. These women saw themselves "adjusting" to the "realities" of "settling down." They said they "left behind" the "adolescent notion" of romantic reverie, along with all the "pressures" to look attractive, talk witty, and feel sexy all the time. They opted for the "more mature comforts" of blissful boredom, often livened up by the hassled serenity of motherhood. But their bliss was barely skin-deep. When I asked them about their relationship with their man, they gave me that "what relationship?" glare and some chilly responses: "We function well together." "I broke him into helping with the kids." "We don't get the chance to talk much, but at least we don't fight." A few faced the facts more jovially, though: "Thank God, he comes home every night because I wouldn't make it on the marriage market today!" Ah, the voices of disillusionment, hidden anger, and sinking self-worth.

But the doubts and dissatisfactions of all these women struck a common disquieting cord: At some point before the process of going began, they felt that their man had stopped treating them the way he used to, and they didn't know why. They were pretty specific about the difference, too.

Most of the men who had been left, either totally or in spirit, hadn't noticed they'd changed – at least not until the possibility was suggested in the interview. No, they had other theories about what happened (see Chapter 7), if they had any at all. The problem was that their theories didn't match the women's. Not that women have cornered the market on Truth. But perhaps Truth isn't the issue here.

If you're concerned with keeping your woman, *her* perceptions are the issue. Some men find it hard to accept a woman's view over their own. But as you'll learn in the next chapter, women are awfully sharp when it comes to psyching out interpersonal situations. Besides, the strongest resisters are destined to be longest running woman-losers.

But there's good news out of all this for you men who want to win with your women. Since women are pretty consistent about what turns them on, turns them off, and drives them away, I can offer you *standard* and *reliable* strategies for keeping your woman. Amid these strategies are also special techniques to keep "special" women, and special techniques to keep your woman special. I can also enlighten you about the standard ways you can *lose* her and her devotion, as well as standard signs that you are. So you'll know exactly how to gauge it if you're in trouble; and if you are, exactly what to do and what not to do to set things right with her again. Yes, women are *that* predictable. You just have to understand what makes them tick and what ticks them off.

By the way, I'm not going to pussyfoot around with you in this book. You're going to hear some tough talk; you've already gotten some. It shouldn't offend you. You're grown men, and I'm talking to you as a friend. I've spent a lot of time around men, and I know you like your talk served up straight, crisp, and a bit salty – not watered down, buttered-up, or sugar-coated. But don't forget I'm a *woman* friend. I want to reach you, because I love you men.

Chapter 1.

Why Keeping Your Woman Is a Problem

You finally found her and won her heart – the girl of your dreams, the love of your life, the woman you've always wanted. Congratulations, Mister! You deserve her, too. But at this point, a lot of you men breathe a sigh of relief and sit back a little too far on your laurels, blindly believing things will *always* stay this way. It's kind of funny – you seem more aware of the winds of change when you're sitting at $20 tables in Vegas.

There's a *new* challenge awaiting you: Now that you *have* her, how do you *keep* her, and *keep her the way you love her*? This challenge is a lot tougher, like the difference between taking the opener and winning the pennant. The key is *consistency*, right?

You men, with your delightful peacock personalities, have a fairly *easy* time *attracting* women. Really. You just don't know how easy because most women play a pretty sly game at the start (and never quite as sly again, do they?), and you put a lot of effort into fluffing up your feathers. Once you attract the Right Woman, winning her heart comes easy, too – easy because you're so *inspired.* For the first – and perhaps last – time in your life, you know intuitively *exactly what a woman wants*. And just as important, you have the *energy* to go out and give her what she wants – love being the best upper available. Romantic dinners (you suddenly learn how to cook gourmet). Hearts and flowers (you know enough to skip the candy since true lovers are seldom hungry). Movies, plays, and concerts of "special meaning" to the two of you. Kites, cards, balloons, banana daiquiris, and whatever little favor reminds you both of that rare, unrelenting reverie.

So why does it relent?

A few weeks, months, or years later, you feel you've laid a "solid foundation" and can go back to those "other things" you feel you've been neglecting. Suddenly, you're as appalled as your squash partner that you missed the last Broncos game. (You were on a wine-and-cheese picnic with your woman.) And you're getting teased by the happy-hour crowd about not hanging out as much as you used to.

"Having your shots between the sheets these days, huh?" You even start to fear you're (gulp!) pussy-whipped. And maybe you've fallen just a bit behind in your work, or so that guilty, ambitious little voice in your head tells you.

Hell, gourmet cooking takes a lot of time. Nice restaurants cost bucks, and you have to wear a tie. And your woman can whip up a fine meal so much faster. Flowers—well, *one bunch* costs the same as two or three six packs. Besides, the florist is out of your way home. Amusements? "Sure, honey, but not 'Terms of Endearment' *again*. How about Eastwood's latest? Or better yet, there's a night game playing in the city...."

Kite strings break. Balloons shrivel up. Daiquiris are too sweet. And cards – well, they're hard to remember to get.

Besides, you figure, there's no *problem* between you and your woman these days, and all that attention you were paying her a little while back ought to hold her for a long time. *You* don't *feel* any differently about her; *certainly* she knows that.

Don't be so sure – not if you want to keep her. She can't read your heart any more easily than you can read her mind. Besides, men and women don't always speak the same language.

In fact, a woman is prone to be downright *suspicious* about the wealth of love you have for her. She's not so sure about that buried treasure you once declared for her. She always seems to be demanding some precious gems of proof. Why can't she just *believe* it's still there for her?

Let's tackle your new challenge – keeping her and keeping her the way you love her – by starting out with why women are such Doubting Tammies about your love. First, we'll step back and look at the big, sometimes ugly, picture of male-female relations. Then we'll telephoto in on what *you* tend to do and *don't* do, usually unwittingly, to make your baby lose the faith.

Do Men Really Love Women?

For some good and some not-so-good reasons, there are a lot of angry women out there. And they've been saying (and publishing) some pretty nasty things about you men, especially over the past fifteen years. They accuse you of treating women like maids, slaves, harlots, and whores; of keeping them repressed, depressed, and oppressed; of bounding and abusing them till you abandon them – that is, being absolute rats.

The milder, more scholarly stuff claims you're simply indifferent. Some of it complains that you think you've got better things to do than attend to your woman. In the *Dialectic of Sex*, for example, Shulamuth Firestone regrets that ". . . women live for love and men live for work." Other feminists, like Lillian Rubin, contend that men and women wind up "ultimate strangers" because men are basically Lone Rangers who reject women's overtures for closeness. Either way, you stand charged with not giving your woman the time and energy she gives you, and deserves.

Whatever their rhetoric, these angry women don't think you give a damn about keeping your woman, except for some creature and carnal comforts. To them, you regard a woman as you do a car: You bargain for the prettiest body with the easiest handling at the lowest price, then give her just enough care to keep her running. You drive her hard for a few years, use up the best of her, and trade up for a younger, sleeker model. (Apologies to you classic car enthusiasts.)

Now, you've got to admit that many women have a *right* to be angry. Sure, their plight has greatly improved over the past forty years. But they're just emerging from a long history of being screwed over in the labor market, kept out of men's most favored jobs, passed over for promotions, and paid less for work that's just as psychologically and mentally taxing as yours (and sometimes physically, too). They've been denied public recognition and power, ownership rights and credit, outside participation, and inside information – all stuff that independent personhood and full citizenship are made of.

In the more personal arena, they've been pinched, pillaged, battered, raped, and indiscreetly impregnated, whether they've asked for it or not. And invariably their cries for equality have been taken less than seriously. There's *no* way that your picking up the dinner tab and opening the door for them are going to make up.

To be fair, *some* of you men have played bullies in this battle of the sexes – many of you without realizing it. (Not that this is an excuse any more than is not knowing the speed limit.) But whether or not you've been hip to the punches you've been pulling, you've obviously had your motives. Understandable ones, too.

A lot of you have a stronger sense of loyalty to your fellow man than your fellow woman. So when a sister threatens *his* interests, you play your brother's keeper. (The problem is that often your fellow woman isn't your neighbor's wife. She's on her own and needs the break as much as he does.)

Others of you have real problems dealing with women as equals. You find them hard to trust (how else did they get tagged "ball-busters" and "man-eaters"?), difficult to take orders from (it's unsettling to see that nurturing softness turn hard-nosed), and, at times, even rather childish (they giggle and chatter together a lot, especially about men.) Women *do* seem "different," like natives of another land. Indeed, they do inhabit a different world from yours, especially when they're young. And like any foreign folk, they can seem too strange to *really like*, too eccentric to *really respect*, too unpredictable to *try* to *understand*, and too threatening to *really accept*. We'll make an expedition down into this sexual chasm in Chapter 3.

But does all this mean that women are too alien for men to *really love*? Or that *men* are too egocentric, insecure, immature, or chauvinistic to really love women? Would they decide to share their life with one were it not for perks like clean clothes, hot meals, and passion-upon-request? Do they want that Special One to be something more special than a nodding head, an eager ear, and a French maid? Do they even care enough about her to *really* want to *keep her*, and more than just keep her around until she wears out?

Those angry women don't think so. A lot of hurt women fear they're right. The rest of the sex at least wonders, especially after a man's wining, dining, and sweet words of pining suddenly stop.

Okay, let's concede that you don't always treat your woman, and other women, the way they deserve; that you do take advantage of their urge to serve; that you resent the energy it can take to deal with them; that you can't fully respect a woman unless she can do what you do twice as well; and that when you do encounter such a woman, you often feel put off.

Now let's look at the rest of the evidence.

Surveys show that *women* are more important to you than *anything* else – more so than your job, your buddies, even the World Series (contrary to the impression men convey at times). When asked what makes you happiest in life, you tend to rank love first, family life second, then friends, sex, and money – pretty much as women do. Furthermore, you say you want companionship and affection first and foremost out of a love relationship, with a partner who is above all trustworthy and intelligent. So much for your locker room lip service to the feather-brained blonde. You'd rather have a javelin-witted Erica Jong or Dorothy Parker.

It might come as a surprise to you that women prioritize exactly the same qualities in a relationship as you do. That should deflate your fears about some gorgeous, money-bagged macho man whisking your woman away.

Another piece of evidence, as if *you* didn't know: Men *go to hell* when their woman leaves them. Their entire world falls apart, often until the next special woman comes along and helps them put it back together. They let their work slide, forego their hobbies, dissolve into depression, and don't even care who won the heavyweight title. Their buddies worry. And even watching The Daily Show doesn't help. You men take it all *very hard*, harder than you'll ever let a woman know.

So, on balance, you men can stand justly accused of all kinds of big and little crimes against women. But not considering them important, not loving them, and not caring about keeping them *aren't* among them.

You say you know that? Yeah, but your woman probably doesn't. And she's the ultimate judge. Given men's previous record with women, you may look a lot guiltier than you actually are. So you have to *prove* your *innocence*.

Ignorance Kills Bliss

So if women are so important to you, and you want so desperately to keep one, how come so many of you so often succeed in losing yours? And men *do* lose their women frequently. Look at the U.S. divorce statistics: an almost 60% strikeout rate. Co-habitators do worst. Less domestic arrangements have an even shorter half-life. And, as we'll see later, it's usually *women* who do the leaving and *men* who *get left*. "Love 'em and leave 'em" may be a male motto, but it's a female modus operandi.

It's not that women are the cold, cruel ball-busters and man-eating tigers that men's castration fantasies make them out to be. Not at all. A lasting, intimate commitment means just as much to them as it does to you. They really *are*, and can continue to be, those soft, cuddly love-kittens who make your dreams come true.

So how come they so often stray – or, if they stick around, turn into scruffy, scrappy cats?

Gentlemen, notwithstanding your strictly honorable intentions in love, you play a major part, more than you know. In fact, that's your *primary* problem; *ignorance* – not arrogance, not indifference, and certainly not malevolence. Just simple ignorance.

Ignorance of what? Three BIG lessons in love: 1. How your woman (vs. you) measures the "success" of your love relationship. (Time to learn another metric system.) 2. How your behavior toward her typically changes, and the effect this has on her. (A little amateur psychology goes a long way.) And 3. How to "translate" her cues about what's bugging her into your own vernacular. (And you thought you met your foreign language requirement years ago!)

Your ignorance is understandable. Most of you were lucky if you knew a woman's anatomy by age 20. They don't offer Women 101 in high school or college: (They don't offer any number of useful courses, like How to Raise Kids, How to Read Insurance Policies, or How to Live These Days on $40,000 a Year.) But consider yourself enrolled now. The course is worth countless credits. This book is your text, and your assignments are to put its lessons into practice. Your woman will administer and grade the tests. Yes, she's tough, but she takes effort and improvement into consideration.

This lesson is just introductory, of course. But it will tell you how you tend to blow it with women and what you need to learn. So, class, let's get down to the subject matter!

Standard Weights and Measures. Your needs and expectations in a love relationship tend to be pretty simple and straightforward. You want a sense of security and permanence with your woman, her tacit loyalty and fidelity, a feeling of laid-back comfort around her, and some notion of teamwork toward common goals. Your idea of "goals" is quite uncomplicated, too: your and your loves ones' health, welfare, and economic well-being.

Not that these needs and hopes are always easy to fulfill. But they are rather basic and elementary, and really quite general, abstract, and on-going. The only way you can measure your success in meeting them is in terms of the problems *you're not having*. If everything seems to be mellow with your woman and around the house, great – you're satisfied. In fact, it doesn't even occur to you to "assess the situation." You just kick back and enjoy it. It's only when *problems crop up* – you think your woman's wandering, your checkbook turns red, your kid's in trouble – that you take stock of things. And sometimes, it's too late.

Your woman has pretty much the same wants and desires as you do. But she defines and operationalizes them much more *complexly* and *concretely* than you do. *She's* looking at *specific, day-to-day* events in your shared world. She's weighing words, analyzing actions, predicting probabilities – checking the love-and-welfare barometer *all the time*. So when she's always asking you how you are, how you feel, where you're at, etc., she's not just being polite or ingratiating. She's taking a reading.

Let's get as specific as she does. You define security and permanence as "no threat to your love on the horizon," even if visibility is poor. But *she's* counting up your tangible dosages of reassurance and recommitment, dividing them by your private time together, and calculating the ratio of this quotient to her security needs (usually a constant). Who says women aren't good at math?

Onward to loyal and fidelity. To *you*, those mean that your woman's *not* betraying you – not running you down in public, not spreading your secrets around, not mocking you behind your back, not taking her love to town, and not deceiving you if she does. All kinds of *"not's."* To *her*, it's not only all the "not's"; it's a lot of affirmative action, too: actively saying *good* things about her in public; showing her affection around other men and especially women; checking in with her during parties; *really* pouring your heart out to her; acting on her advice; taking her out for romantic evenings (no, not just night baseball); surprising her with cards and flowers; whispering sweet something's in her ear (there must be 50 ways to say "I love you."); and, by all means, taking her to bed (or wherever) with you as often as you can. As you can well imagine, she has quite a calculus for figuring your fidelity quotient: add up the affirmative actions, subtract the number of "not's" committed (which are weighted more heavily), and divide the difference by how attractive she thinks she is. So if she thinks she's a 9, you need more affirmatives and fewer "not's" to score a decent F.Q. than if she thinks she's a 5.

Now to the concept of comfort. To you, it means you don't feel odd when you burp, fart, pig out, get sloppy drunk, crack dirty jokes, parade around in ragged underwear, or otherwise act like a slob every once in a while. Your woman probably doesn't push comfort *this* far. In fact, her notion of comfort with you may be too subtle for you to realize that she needs the reassurance. *She* wants to know if you still love her without her face made up and her hair combed; if you still would if she gained 10 pounds; if you still will when her breasts droop, her hair grays, and her face wrinkles. Maybe she's even asked. And you probably gave her one of your "there, there" smiles and a curt "of course." But you might not have come off too convincing if you didn't seem to have thought about the issues or appreciated the seriousness of her concerns.

Her notion of teamwork is different, too – with the accent on specific *work* for those general team goals. She's judging your efforts to carry the ball on the less glamorous plays: through a stack of dirty dishes, into a pile-up of laundry, and through the blows of bill-paying. She also wants credit for catching *your* difficult passes – like for closing her eyes to that second-string flirtation in your life or mounting a strong defense when your job or reputation is on the line. Granted her game goes by a more complicated set of rules than yours. But if you don't play it, she may exercise her free-agent option.

So the lesson boils down to: Understand that her love metric is much finer and more precise than yours, her accounting more frequent, and her computations much more complex. But you don't have to be a math whiz to measure up. Just don't be guilty of short-weighing her.

The Falling Rate of Interest. Remember when you were first forming your partnership? You really wooed your woman's business! You projected steady growth, record profit sharing, and lavish returns of your interest. You were a helluva salesman with all the right moves – but a sincere, inspired one, as I portrayed you at the very beginning of the chapter. So she made the big investment, designating you sole trustee of her heart. And you paid her sky-high dividends. Mutual interests were booming.

With business rolling, you turned more and more to those "other things" we talked about and quietly delegated most intimacy-management responsibilities to her. After all, she showed such a natural flair for them. And, she was willing to put in longer hours on them than you did. It was a *rational* decision. And a *just* one, you felt, because you'd continue to pay her, if not with as high a rate of your interest, with "stock options." That is, you promised her a stable, secure, long-term partnership to build her "portfolio" around: You'd always come home to her.

Now, from *her* point of view, you did something quite different. First, by cutting back on your interest, you manipulated the business cycle from boom to bust, just like the Feds. And why? *She* didn't feel that inflation was eating away at the value of your passions. Then you dumped all the managerial burdens on her, while you pursued other and, to her, less profitable ventures. Finally, you had the gall to substitute stock options for more immediate returns. "Hell," she's thinking, "I *need* your steady, high interest just to live in the romantic style to which you've made me accustomed. Stock options won't make me rich unless I threaten to withdraw my investment and make *you* come running after me."

You wouldn't want her to pull *that* speculative play, would you? Or has she already, you say? Sure, it's bad for long-term business planning. But that may be her only way to rally your interest rate. *She* fears that she might have soaked her heart's savings into the Brooklyn Bridge.

What you have to realize is that when you start paying out less than she's giving, and she in turn starts protecting her accounts by investing less, selling out, or otherwise jerking the bottom out of the market, *your* stock goes down. You're not checking the exchange listings every day the way she is. But that booming partnership that you once worked so hard to set up isn't as bullish as it used to be. In fact, when you find yourself in a life pinch someday, you may discover there's little left to draw off the home account. Like when you have to break the bad news about your lost job or the other woman, and you need a loan of faith from your woman, you may find yourself short of collateral.

The purpose of this economics lesson is not to discourage your romantic entrepreneurial spirit, but to encourage sound business practices: Make good on the returns you've promised, or renegotiate them. Avoid those sudden short falls. Do your fair half of the managing. Why should you trust anyone else to run your most important affair? Finally, stay on top of the market; ask your woman for a stock quote every once and a while. You have a big investment to protect, too.

Parlez-vous Womanese? You're probably not very fluent. And if you're not, you might as well set up housekeeping in the Tower of Babel. You men have a sense of the language gap, too. In fact, you tend to be more dissatisfied with the level of communication in love relationships than are women. You're even inclined to blame yourself. Men generally feel they're less of a love-linguist than do women.

Women probably *are* better. After all, they're the less powerful group, and some aspire to break into the man's world of high-powered careers, sports, big money, and the like. So they *have* to understand *you*. They have to be bisexually-lingual. (Have you ever heard of *men* wanting to "break into" the *woman's* world? Actually, you'd be perfectly welcome. Think for a second – why doesn't the idea appeal?)

It may be true that some of the more timid and fawning females speak "manese" with a distractingly heavy accent ("That account seems a bit weak to me.") and have some trouble with your idioms ("That running back sure made a fast break.") And many women dilute a lot of their declarative statements with a questioning little rise in pitch (for example, in her dialect, "The ref should call clipping, shouldn't he?" versus proper manese, "Clipping, you sonavabitch!") But most women do a halfway decent job picking up your lingo, at least in the "masculine" arenas where you have one.

There's *one crucial* arena, though, where you don't have much more than a few prehistoric grunts and mumbles – and that's the arena of *feelings* and *relationships*.

The basic problem is that where womanese makes many fine distinctions and nuances, you don't. It's like the Eskimos, who have over twenty different words for various types of snow, meeting with the Aztecs, who have one word for white-stuff-on-top-of-the-mountains, and talking about winter weather.

For instance, you call a "good buddy" anyone from the plumber-you-can-trust, to the nice-guy-you-run-into-at-your-hangout-once-a-month, to the army-buddy-from-another-world-you-would-have-laid-down-your-life-for, to your closest life-long friend.

Women, on the other hand, have "friends," "good friends," "close friends," and "best friends" – all hierarchically ranked and labeled.

Or "love" – now, *there's* a five-cent to five-thousand-dollar word. When you say you "love" a woman, you can mean want-to-go-to-bed-with, want-to-have-a-fling-with, want-to-have-a-real-affair-with, want-to-marry, or wish-I-could. You can even mean that you just want to be her dear friend, or that you find her too crystalline beautiful to dare to defile. Then there are the totally different ways you love your sister, aunt, cousin, and, last but always first, your mother. Trouble arises when you use the unqualified word "love" to an unrelated female whom you *don't* want to marry or whom you wish you could but won't. (Or am I opening up old wounds? Sorry.)

Anyway, women are pretty careful about this crazy thing called love. To them, it means pretty serious business. If they *don't*, they'll tell you they like you, admire you, are fond of you, care about you, want a fling with you, want an affair with you, or thanks but no thanks. They're pretty specific. And they expect you to be, too. Since *your* language doesn't speak to the issue, shouldn't you use *theirs*? Isn't that why we borrow from the Italians in music, the French in diplomacy, and the Germans in science?

That's not the only communication gap, however. It's not only *what* you say, but *how* you say it, too. When your woman is perturbed at you, she may cry, nag, or bitch. To *you*, all of these are a sign that she's "lost it," that she's in an irrational state of mind and is not to be believed. Why? Because if *you* or another *man* cried, nagged, or bitched over the issue, you'd have perfectly sound reason to think that. Not that you never feel like letting it out in those ways. But as a male, you've been taught harshly *not to*. Better you punch out a window or nose, or insult someone about his manhood.

Not so with your woman. In fact, quite the opposite. She was taught that crying, nagging, and bitching are perfectly *rational* (though not necessarily the most effective) ways to express frustration and anger. Crying to her is just a harmless release of emotions, and one with dramatic value. (It's like Italians gesturing to each other after a close shave in traffic. Eh, no grossa problema.) Saying things more than once (what you call nagging) multiplies the chances of your hearing her grievance and responding. (It's a hit-or-miss technique, but you'll have to admit that it does work sometimes.) And speaking rapidly at a high pitch (translation: bitching) is to *her* just a natural physio-logical by-product of her heightened impatience – the same as *your* speaking more slowly at a lower pitch while you're trying to keep your lid on. So when she "carries on" in her feverishly feminine way, her head may be pretty cool. Give her a fair hearing, and *your* temperature may drop. If she's *really* "losing it", she'll probably square off like a man, because she's learned *that's* taboo for *her*.

There's still another, even more subtle language chasm. While womanese is *specific* about feelings, women don't always use it *literally*, by the dictionary. So sometimes you may have to translate one word into another.

It's not that your woman is trying to throw you off. Usually she's *trying* to be as honest, direct, and effective as she knows how. But for deep emotional and "political" reasons, she may not say exactly what she *really* means.

Too typically, a woman plaintively claims, "You don't love me the same anymore. What's wrong? How have I let you down?" And you too typically don't have the smoggiest notion of what she's talking about. You love her the same as *ever*, and *nothing* is wrong. As far as you can see, you've been treating her just as royally (or as poorly) as ever. If your woman claims you don't love her anymore, you have to translate her jargon into the plain, awful truth: *"I* don't love *you* the same way anymore. I can't face what's wrong alone. *You* let *me* down."

Don't panic. Turn the tables on her. Ask her how much truth there is to the translation and how awful it is. Give her time to cry. After all, your sensitivity may shock her a bit, and she'll need a few moments to dry out her thoughts. But she'll tell you what's *really* bugging her if you answer her off-the-wall question with the right-on one.

But why, if *she's* doubting *her* love for *you*, does she question *you* about *your* love for *her*? Well, it all goes back to "Do Men Really Love Women?" Women are never quite sure to begin with, so they keep going back to the question like homing pigeons, even when they have the urge to fly south. But even more to the point, women have been taught to be just *plain* pigeons – *not* to follow their own good *offensive* instincts in the battle of the sexes. They've been told that "nice girls" only play defense. So if you attack, abuse, or abandon them, they know it's okay to fight back, even to call foul.

But if you play it cool and "within the rules," yet they're *still* disenchanted, they don't know *who* or *what* to fight. What they'd *really* like to do is change the *rules*. Men get too many time-outs, and women knock themselves silly for too low stakes. But they're not well organized enough to take control of the league.

No, in their sense of powerlessness and self-doubt, they only take the offense against *themselves*. They wonder what *they've* done wrong to lose *your* love, when deep down inside, they know exactly what *you've* done wrong to lose *their* love.

So, to recap this foreign-language lesson: When on woman's turf, speak the language your woman does. And you don't have to duck around like an illegal alien; you'll be naturalized upon request. Be careful, too, about diagnosing your woman as "hysterical." One man's insanity is a woman's rationality, and vice versa. Finally, help your woman speak her own language more clearly. She may tend to mix up her you's and I's, especially if she's upset with you, in which case you'd *better* get the message straight.

Chapter 2.

Why Keeping Your Woman Is Your *Responsibility*

Now that you know a little more about what you don't know, you may be wondering why *you* have to know anything at all. Hell, if *women want* to be kept, why don't *they* just keep themselves keepable and stick around? In other words, why should *you* be bothered?

If that's your attitude, you're not the only freeloader around. It's pretty widespread among even the most "socially conscious" of you (who may be the last to want to admit it.) A while back, I walked into a session at the American Psychological Association convention on whether men can understand women. The huge room was packed far beyond capacity and overflowed out every door. If you didn't know what was going on, you would have thought they were giving away perfume, diet pills, or vibrators. *Women*, wall-to-wall women, outnumbering men by at least 3 to 1. I didn't think there were that many female psychologists in the whole country. And God knows where the men were – maybe at the session on neuro-ocular maladaptations in the stressed male mouse. (Now you tell me honestly, what's more interesting and important: women, or a twitch in Mickey's eye?)

Anyway, a lot of excuses got tossed about for why men don't bother to study or even understand women: Men feel like they're on alien territory; they equate "humankind" with *man*kind; and the bottom line, as the more powerful sex, men don't have to understand women. Women *can't* leave you, right? Aren't *they* the more romantic and emotionally dependent? Don't *they* have more to *gain* from a man and more to *lose* without him? After all, *they* have the kids and have to look out for them. So don't *they* suffer worst if it ends? And aren't *men* the "natural" ramblers anyway?

Okay, this will sober you up: wrong, wrong, wrong, wrong, wrong – let's see, I lost count. But you're right on one score: Women *do* generally (but not always) get the kids, and they stand to lose *big* economically. Almost no one will pay them the same as they do you, even for the *same* skills and the *same* education on the *same* job. Then only half you daddies follow through on your full child support payments, which rarely cover all the costs of raising a child.

No wonder that half the families below the "official poverty level" (and that's genuine destitution) are headed by females. A woman can't *marry* as downwardly mobile as she winds up if she gets herself *un*married.

But you know what? Women leave their men in droves *anyway*. This means things must be pretty bad when they do, and maybe they're not even as emotionally dashed and deprived without a man as you might think. So let's get back to that list of wrong's.

Now, I'm going to give you some damn *good* reasons why you *have* to bother to keep your woman. While you men have the power advantage in the economic, political, physical, and just about any other front, you *don't* really have it on the *love* front. (And dare I bring up the sexual to the over-45 group?) This isn't just my opinion; it's *scientific fact*.

1. Men Are More in Love with Love.

Think about it. When was the last time a woman brought *you* flowers, or wrote *you* an impassioned love letter, or waxed poetically on the ways she worshipped *you*? It happens – so do eclipses – but not in the regular scheme of things. A woman is particularly likely to play it coy early in a love relationship, which is when you're laying on the romance for all it's worth. *After* you successfully woo her, *then* you probably get some reassuring samples of her sentimentality. But she tends toward more *practical* demonstrations. She'll patch your jeans with a heart or write "I love you!" on a shopping list. I mean, you can't *wear* flowers, and you can't plan dinners with a love letter.

Somehow, though, you men are more than happy with *any* romantic display you get from your woman. You almost never complain, at least not as long as sexual displays are available. (A big problem is that some women don't consider sex "practical" enough.) Even in bed, you're rarely the one who requests words of endearment (dirty talk, maybe). You're more likely to be reciting them to her.

No, contrary to the misguided myth of the mushy-hearted female, *men* are the true romantics of the species. And it's because you get off on romantic notions – like the thrill of the chase and the challenge of unrequited love – that you can survive so contently on a less-than-lavish diet of lovey-dovey from your woman.

That's quite an assertion to make – that *you*'re more romantic than women as a rule. A lot of you men may already be nodding in agreement. (You can't forget all that wooing you wasted on some well-sculpted iceberg.) But some of the *women* out there may need some convincing, especially those who haven't had a man go mad over them in a while.

And men *do* go *mad* over women. Psychologists have thought up questions to measure people's romanticism. Ask yourself, for example, how much do you believe that love at first sight really happens, that true love lasts forever, and that true love can overcome racial, religious, cultural, and economic differences? Those chuckles in the audience are probably coming from *women*. Men are more inclined to agree with those idyllic ideals, and they're the ones applauding.

Further, a man's sense of attachment to his woman is more romantic than is a woman's to her man. *Both* sexes see attachment as being sexually exclusive, spending time together, believing the relationship will endure, and feeling intimate and close with your loved one. But men also include "feeling romantic" about the relationship, as well as getting satisfaction from it. Women, as a group, don't pick out either. (That also must mean they'll go longer in an *un*satisfactory relationship.)

Men follow through in their actions too. They fall in love more quickly and more eagerly, with a wider range of partners, and with greater faith in the love lasting. In fact, one might say that their devotion is less discriminating, even promiscuous, because they're even more likely to fall head over heels for a randomly matched blind date.

And when they fall, they go boom. They report stronger attraction to and love for their woman than their woman does for them. So they're absorbing the heart-breaking, ego-shattering risks, putting their passions on the line *first*. But that's only at the start of the relationship. If the love flies, she catches up, and he comes a bit more to his senses. Still, there's no doubt about it: Women are decidedly slow, cautious, and very wary about getting involved, and definitely more discriminating about who with.

I can almost hear you cynics snickering that men just give their hearts to get head. Not so. Their intentions are at least as pure as they are prurient – if anything, innocent and idealistic to a fault.

Men's #1 reason for falling in love is because they're in love with *love*. In other words, they do it for the romantic reverie.

So, men, if you want it so much, and you go through such heroic lengths to get it, it falls largely on *you* to keep it and keep her the prize you fought for.

2. *Men Have More to Gain in Love and More to Lose without It.*

Romantic reverie notwithstanding, you men have a lot of starkly *rational* reasons to catch and keep a woman – I daresay, a lot more rational than some of *her* reasons for sticking with you. Put simply, your quality of life improves tremendously with a woman's touch.

For starters, you probably eat better.

As a bachelor, you may master a few Saturday night specialties, like the Pope's Lasagna and Five-Alarm Chili. But after spending Sunday cleaning up after yourself, you probably got your daily sustenance from the local bar and grill, or delved into your ever-shrinking stash of frozen dinners and canned goods. Well, man does not live by hot dogs, Tater Tots, and Franco American spaghetti alone. Certainly not well. Maybe not for long.

What greater pleasure is there in life than to come home to a real home-cooked meal seasoned with a woman's love? (Okay, maybe truly gourmet sex.) Even if your shapely chef isn't particularly creative in the kitchen, she's attentive to your culinary likes and dislikes. And in this health-hip day and age, she probably serves as your own personal dietician (too much, you say?), counting your calories, cutting down your saturated fats and sugars, and regulating your junk-food and booze intake. She even cooks for your friends and works hardest on Sundays and holidays. No doubt, you'd have to put on a tie and pay a lot of money to get her efforts in a restaurant.

Of course, before she met you, she most likely was eating just as well on her own.

Another big plus: You've probably got less housework to do. Not that you were doing a great deal before, but eventually you'd run out of clean dishes, clean socks, and the stomach to walk into your bathroom. The solutions were almost as unpleasant as the problems, weren't they?

With all due respect to you beloved exceptions out there, the vast majority of men do *very little* housework once they're living with a woman, and no doubt less than they were doing before. While men are pretty good about picking up a few groceries, mowing the lawn, and trying their hand at heavy repair jobs, the lion's share of the household humdrum *still* falls on the lioness: cooking, dishes, laundry, ironing, picking-up-after, vacuuming, dusting, polishing, waxing, sweeping, scrubbing, scouring, sanitizing, sewing, plant-watering, gardening, window-washing, miscellaneous wiping, and all the less-than-delightful tasks of child-raising (a list of which might make you lose your lunch). A lot of these jobs would tire a construction crew.

But, hell, you say, a lot of them *don't have* to be done – not so often, not so "perfectly." The dishes can sit till mañana. Making love a couple of times doesn't make the sheets a public health hazard. And you don't have to "see your face" in something to call it clean (except the mirror). You're right. If your woman keeps house to the standards of a hospital operating room – and a few do – you need to help her with her filth phobia, not with the laundry. The trouble is, the more "time-saving" cleaning devices advertisers push, the cleaner "nice" homes are supposed to be.

There are several well documented figures floating around on the average number of hours per week wives spend doing housework. But the most conservative puts the full-time housewife's at 53 hours and the working wife's at over 20, plus 5% to 10% more time with each child. It's not that the typical working wife gets more help, either from a maid or her husband. She just bites the bullet on housekeeping standards and does less.

In any case, when a woman picks up with a man, she picks up a lot more housework along the way. When a *man* picks up with a *woman*, he somehow sloughs off the bulk of it. A dear friend of mine didn't realize how much until his working wife left him. Six months later, he confided he "couldn't keep up with the back-breaking demands" of his small six-room house, and he hired a maid.

What else do you get out of a life with a woman? You might not believe this, but spending power! Yes, indeed, contrary to all those myths about the women wearing the pants in the family, men wind up making most of the expense decisions. I don't mean the penny-wise ones about what brand of toothpaste or green beans to buy. Or that bothersome business about what to get who for the holidays. Or even what shade of off-white to paint the living room. (Do *you* really care?) I mean the solemn, significant, really fun-to-make decisions – like what house or apartment to live in, what car to drive, what computer to buy, and where to invest your (and her) money. You usually have the last word, even if she keeps the books. With her working, too, you get even more disposable income to dispose of.

But, you say, she *wants* me to make these decisions. She claims she has no head for investments, no knowledge of cars, no interest in real estate. It's true that many women shy away from these areas. In general, women tend to worry more about personal finances and investments, so they would just as soon abdicate the responsibility to you. (And, unfortunately, they jab at you later if you screw up. That's the cost of your power.)

Still, that doesn't spoil the fun for you. Even if you haven't *grabbed* the power, you still have it. And it's sweet.

Speaking of aphrodisiacs, sex is one of those big gains from your woman that you wouldn't want to lose.

Not that you couldn't get it elsewhere. But isn't having to get all spiffed up, put on the Hollywood smoothy routine, and engage in hours, if not weeks of mating rituals to get it a bit of a *hassle* – even for sex? And then , what kind of sex do you get? You're nervous. So is she. You get off too quick or too late or not at all. Or you're too drunk to remember. She gets into some Kama Sutra position, and you don't know what to do. You'll never know if she *really* turned on and got off or not, and you hate to ask. The next day, you frantically search your pockets for her name and phone number, and yourself for signs of disease. She may be wondering if you still "respect" her. You may be worrying if you still respect *yourself.*

Who needs it? Not if you can get a higher quality version from your woman in the comfort of your own home, and for no more pomp and circumstance than some loving words, a passionate kiss, and a smoldering gaze.

Okay, okay, it isn't always *that* easy. Sometimes you happen to pick a bad time. But usually it's *you* who picks the time, which is a nice privilege, isn't it? Until they get a little older, most women are still hesitant to initiate. ("What if he can't get it up?" "Will he think I'm a whore if I come on to him?" "Will he resent me for playing *his* role?) Or they're too preoccupied with all their housework and child-caring to let such a devilish delight enter their mind. (Too bad.)

Nor is sex with your woman always *that* great. As a number of you put it, sometimes sex is steak and sometimes it's hamburger. Some of you more finicky eaters even occasionally prefer new hamburger to a steady diet of the same filet. But at least with your very own woman, you can take comfort in knowing what's on the menu, and knowing you won't *starve*.

Even beyond square meals, services rendered, spending power, and steady sex, you get to enjoy the freedom of *intimacy*. Yes, I said "freedom" – the freedom to slip off your gray flannel disguise and really run *naked* with someone.

"Intimacy" has a somewhat bum rep because we think of it so often as "sharing problems." So you come home from work, gripe about the traffic, skewer with your boss, and confide how unhappy you are on the job. Yeah, that's intimacy, sort of. We all need a dumping ground for our hassles and insecurities, and mates often provide the most patient, sympathetic, and available trash site.

That's not the *best* of intimacy, though. The best is being able to come home from work, boast on about the coup you pulled off at the office, and confide how "hot" you think you are in your career. Really now, would you display such self-congratulatory glee in front of your *friends*? But your woman is practically prancing around with pompoms for even your smallest victories.

Intimacy is fun, too. We get away with some pretty crazy shenanigans, things we wouldn't *dream* of trying on *anyone* else – not even our mother. One man I know gets his dinner-time jollies chasing his woman around the table and pinching her ass with kitchen tongs. Another highly articulate friend of mine winds down from a hard day of public speaking by babbling with his wife in baby talk. If she doesn't feel quite like a two-year-old that evening, she mothers him, sometimes right into a seduction. Then there's a distinguished gentlemen I know who, rather than simply ask about dessert, transforms into a wild-eyed, moronic Cookie Monster in an uncontrollable sugar frenzy. His woman obligingly plays "keeper" and leads him like a pet to the available sweets stash. (My reassurances of strict confidentiality to my trusting friends!) Intimacy with your woman can get so ribald and ridiculous that it makes a Super Bowl booze bust look like a church service.

Of course, your woman gets all the delights of intimacy with *you*, too; she has her wild streak, too. It's not with just *anyone* she'll share who's-sleeping-with-who gossip or debate names for her new vibrator.

But there is one definite difference between the two of you: *Men* are more *dependent* on their woman for intimacy than women are on their men. Why? Because women routinely talk more about personal, emotional stuff with their friends than you guys tend to. And when you *do* need to share a burden with a friend, you're just as likely to seek out a *female* – if not *your* woman, *a* woman. Women are often easier to talk to, right? They listen better and more sympathetically. They ask questions. They see subtle nuances and offer new angles on a situation. They share their *own* stuff with *you* (so you don't feel you're the only jerk in a jam). And they don't push suspiciously simple solutions (like "There's nothing you can do but break up.") No, they'll give you a veritable computer analysis of *possible* strategies to take, depending upon your goal priorities, tactical ethics, time line, and whatever other factors you're able to feed into their system. You can practically hear their minds whirring.

Of course, women perform these services for *each other*, too – all the time. And then they can turn to the men who have been turning to them for the "male point of view." So for any given personal problem, a woman may collect a mental stack of analyses to work with. Along the way, she's enjoyed all kinds of intimate experiences with different people.

You men are more reserved to begin with. Then you tend to congregate at business lunches, on basketball courts, and in Monday Night Football bars, which aren't the best places for a private tête-à-tête. None of the other men around brings up their personal problems, except a few standard ones, like power struggles at work. You might even start to think you're the *only* man with any. But you can bet your 401k you're not. It's just that you men don't *get* the chance or *make* the chance for heart-to-heart chats with each other. Unless you start meeting your buddies in quiet lounges, at coffee klatches, and in powder rooms, you *need* your women to fill the gap.

Because of all these benefits, men *with* a woman are *healthier* than those without in practically every way imaginable. Those *with* one get sick less often, have fewer traffic accidents, and suffer less depression, paranoia, neurosis, and stress. They get into trouble less, commit fewer crimes, commit suicide less, get better jobs, and make more money. The bottom line is that they live *longer* and *happier* lives – longer even than religious celibates. (It seems that sex not only keeps you young; it keeps you *alive*.) Men seem to know that a woman is good for them, too. Divorced and widowed men remarry at a higher rate than single men marry to begin with – and as soon as they can. In fact, half of the divorced men who get another woman to the altar do it within three years of their divorce. God knows how many others just move in with one. Yes, it's so nice to have a woman around the house.

Now, you ask, aren't *women with a man* similarly better off than are women *without*? Well, frankly, no. On most matters, having a man around the house makes no difference. Women still drive the same way, and those who work neither gain nor lose in pay or position. It *is* absolutely true that since they share in their men's fatter paychecks, they enjoy a higher standard of living. And if they have kids, they have a more active social life than if they're separated or divorced. It's also true that married women *say* they are happier than do single women, especially separated and divorced women. But maybe that's because money *does* buy some happiness, or because women are *taught* to think they can't be happy without a man. There's lots of evidence that blurs the picture of their marital bliss.

Feminist Flo Kennedy coined the line: "A woman without a man is like a fish without a bicycle." I believe that view is full of seaweed myself. But it is interesting that *single* women have *higher* mental health overall than do married ones – less depression, less passivity, and fewer phobias and neuroses. They don't run to the doctor or get hooked on prescription drugs so often either. In fact, "the happy housewife" we see on commercials seems to be the *least* so off screen. They're *twice* as likely as working wives to be bummed out by anxiety and worry, loneliness, and feelings of worthlessness.

Wives aren't as healthy as their hubbies, either. They're more prone to nervousness, insomnia, nightmares, headaches, and all manner of nasty stress symptoms. On the other hand, single, divorced, and widowed women are *more* mentally healthy than are *men* in the same boat.

So there sure does seem to be something about marriage and its equivalents that work a whole lot more in a *man's* favor than a woman's. To be totally fair, then, perhaps keeping your love nest intact is more *your* responsibility than your woman's. And it may be, because most men don't carry it out, that women more often fly the coop than do men.

3. Women Are More Likely to Leave.

Yes, chances are that your woman is harder to keep than you are. Of course, after comparing women's mating gains to men's, it makes a bit more sense.

It's not that women are less committed or involved than you men are – actually quite the contrary in most cases. But women *do* have higher expectations and are frankly more demanding and critical of relationships. So they're more easily frustrated and disappointed than you are. Given their lower boiling points, their love vaporizes faster than a man's. That's why they're more likely to turn off the relationship than you are.

Women have all kinds of reasons for wanting out. They get very particular and analytical about them, too. They cite *differences* with their man – most often, differences in interests, intelligence, and ideas about love and marriage – and *better alternatives*, especially for greater independence and, sad to say, another man.

When *men* play the breaker-upper, their reasons aren't usually so sharp and clear, nor so numerous. Frequently they're just less involved than their woman and grow vaguely bored with the whole affair. But it's a rare man who simply wants to go back to the playboy pace of living. In fact, more often than women, men opt out of a relationship because they can't be with their loved one *enough*.

For the typical relationship, though, the best predictor of its longevity is how much the *woman* loves her man. So if you want to know how gracefully your relationship is aging, ask your woman how *she's* feeling about *you*. If you want it to last, learn how to keep her love alive and well.

4. *Men Take Break-ups Harder.*

If you ever suffered through a bitter parting, and took vengeful consolation believing that at least she felt as miserable as you did, well, I hate to be the one to tell you, but she probably didn't.

Wouldn't you know that the more romantic of the exes winds up the more broken-hearted? Whether the man was *more or less* involved in the relationship than his woman, he's *still* usually hit harder. He sinks into deeper loneliness and depression and clings to the flickering love light more tightly. When men are so in love with love, it's hard for them to give it up even when they're less in love with their woman. So, often around break-up time, they suddenly play the Great Conciliator, devising rose-colored ways to resolve differences and abruptly softening demands they've been making of their woman. When this last-minute fix-up effort fails, they feel more regretful than she does that their love didn't get another go-around.

Of course, in the typical case where the man's dumped, he's even *worse* off. He's also shocked, crushed, baffled, mystified, incredulous that his love was unrequited. He feels betrayed, powerless, emasculated, anything but eager to start getting it on with women again. All those myths of vaginal jaws, connubial nutcrackers, and searing sirens come back to haunt him. If his ex-hex sweetly suggests, "But we can still be friends, honey," he'll just as soon warm up to a rattlesnake.

While you men are crying into your bourbon and putting your fists through doors, what are all the abandoned and abandoning women doing? Well, they're crying into their pillows and knocking on their friends' doors for sympathy. But they typically take a cooler, more practical approach to the whole erstwhile affair: Okay, it's over. Let's hide his pictures, stash his letters, and let go of the old hopes and dreams. Let's have no regrets and hold no grudges. The relationship was a good experience. It taught me A, B, C about love and never to do X, Y, Z again. If he didn't love me enough, maybe he's a goddamn fool and I wouldn't want him anyway. But he might make a nice friend.... Well, it's time for a new hair style, some new clothes, a "new look" to pick me up...I think I'll call up Amy and see if she can fix me up with someone this weekend.

Let's not come away with the impression that women find breaking up no more traumatic than selling their old car. They get terribly lonely and depressed, too. The more fragile egos wind up shattered. And in today's mate market, where females so outnumber males, many women fear that their last man may have been their last chance. Those who want to have babies, especially if they're playing Beat the Biological Clock, have to put off or put away that dream as well.

It's just that women approach broken hearts like any other injury or illness. They take more *rational* measures to promote their emotional recovery, much as we all do when we're sick to hasten our *physical* recovery. Only the prescriptions are very different. The *last* thing you do for a broken heart is to stay in bed and take downers.

There's lots of other reasons why you men are more broken up by break-ups. Granted you're less likely to want and initiate one. But you're also less likely to see one coming, so you're less prepared. It strikes unexpectedly, like a hard ball out of left field, and leaves you dazed. You might say, how are you supposed to know it's coming if *she's* the one hurling it? Well, it's funny, but *women* usually see it coming and ready themselves for the impact even when their man is pitching. They routinely scan the emotional field and cultivate their peripheral vision. They look for little signs of his sagging interest: distractedness, forgetfulness, less eye (and other) contact, fewer talks, shorter sentences spoken in a flatter voice. You see, soon-to-be-lost lovers give themselves away, but you have to keep a sharp eye out for every play.

Sometimes men *spot* a problem – hell, their woman may have been hounding them about it – but they won't *confront* it. Don't take this personally now, but it's pretty typical in intimate relationships that a woman wants to discuss a conflict into the ground and gets bitchy and resentful over it; while a man either explodes and forgets it or tries to avoid it by denying its importance, discrediting her perceptions, refusing to *really* talk about it, or leaving the scene entirely. Neither sex has the greatest strategy, and together they escalate a cold war that no one ever wins. But let's be practical. Since *she's* the hawk, she's more inclined to make that first strike and blow you out of her waters.

It's tragic that so many men take it like a surprise attack. They had plenty of warning. Their woman practically nagged them to negotiate. But either they wouldn't attend peace talks in good faith, or they walked out on them.

Once the bomb goes off, no matter who dropped it, men don't have as many close allies to help them rebuild their world either. Remember my saying how women enjoy more intimate friendships, and then have a Salvation Army to turn to after a disaster? Really close friends offer more than sympathy; they also give you practical advice and emotional support for your recovery and reconstruction. Without them, most men remain in ruins much longer.

Of course, the whole idea of this book is to help you prevent getting nuked in the first place. You can less afford it emotionally than The Other Side can. And she wants a blissful coexistence as much as you do.

What About Her?

Some of you must be thinking, hell, why should *I* have to take *all* the responsibility and make *all* the effort to keep her? Read on. You don't, and you shouldn't be expected to.

The problem is that too many men take *too little* responsebility and make *too little* effort – far less than half – to keep the love torch burning. And you owe at least half the fuel, especially since you love *love* so deeply, benefit so much from it, and suffer so badly if it goes – all more so than women usually do. Still, if I were writing *How to Keep Your Man* (I might), I wouldn't bother to tell women why the task was their responsibility or why they should care. They *know* why, and they're eager to learn how. In fact, you men are fairly easy to keep, but you're a real challenge to keep you the way your woman loves you!

It's not that you men are irresponsible or don't care. But you tend *not* to see your relationship with your woman as an *ongoing project*, like your job, your finances, or your kids. You have to, though, because *she* does, and it is ongoing. For sure it's *not* like your car, which needs no more than a little routine maintenance unless it breaks down.

So if you accept your relationship as a *joint* project and set out to keep your woman an active, happy partner, *she* owes you plenty: loving, grateful responses to your efforts; a gentle approach to conflicts; a passionate interest in sex (with you, of course); the freedom (within limits) to do your own thing, or the interest in doing it with you; the encouragement to pursue your personal goals and feasible dreams; and that same alluring, together woman you fell in love with, only more so than ever.

Yes, *you* do *your* part, and chances are *she'll* do *all* this for you, at least *better* than she's been doing it, if she's not already doing it beautifully. The more energy you put into keeping her, the more you'll *want* to keep her and the more likely you *will*.

It's simple physics, gentlemen. Just as countless little slights and stabs can set a relationship on a downward spiral, some moderate strokes and salves can send it skyward. What goes down *can* come back up, if you get past the inertia.

However, even physics predicts in probabilities (though it does beat the odds at a craps table), and this is not a book on how to *manipulate* your woman into being or doing *anything*. If you honestly and faithfully put this book's advice into practice and get disappointing results, consider these possibilities: Your woman may be *very* unusual, beyond the "Special Cases" I analyze in Chapter 12. Ask her what in the world she wants and take notes. Or perhaps the situation is hopeless, and you've either lost her already or ought to let her go, a situation discussed in Chapter 13. Or, at the risk of alienating my sisters' affections, maybe she's not *worth* keeping. It's a mighty rare woman who's so begrudging, dense, or defensive that she doesn't pick up on or warm up to her man's displays of love.

But if she doesn't, she may need professional help, in which case, she needs to get it. Or maybe you don't need *her*. A good man *deserves* a responsive woman. And *you* must be a good man, or you wouldn't have read this far.

Chapter 3.

Viva la Difference and End the Battle of the Sexes

Remember when you first discovered that girls were different from boys? When was it? When you first watched Mommy change Lil' Sis's diaper? Or when you toddled in on Mommy's bath? Or when you and a little friend ducked behind the bushes and pulled down your pants? (It wasn't the last time, was it?) I've never been quite the same since I accidently eyed my playmate Bobby going potty – standing up, holding "this thing" in his hands. I wanted to ask questions, but he barely knew how to talk.

Shocking to be sure, but all we'd tripped on was the tip of the iceberg. A few years later, girls seemed *so different*, so obviously from another galaxy, that you wanted nothing to do with them. Not until you discovered the pleasures of intergalactic exploration.

But still, girls were stranger than science fiction. First they'd turn up their noses to your attention. Then they'd act boy-crazy. Then they'd get coy. One Saturday night they would spread their legs. The next, they would clamp shut. *Then* they'd want (gulp) commitment. But a month later they wouldn't go out with you. Suddenly, God help you, you fell in love with one. And she with you, or so you thought, until just as suddenly she dumped you.

Man, *what is it with females?*

Well, it's no wonder they seem so confusing. We've made up all kinds of contradictory stereotypes about them. We all "know" that they cry and carry on and get so emotional; they're submissive, dependent, and passive, even sort of dim-witted, naïve, impulsive, and not-too-competent; and, *of course*, they're shy about sex. But we also know they can be a despotic Lucy; they aggressively make demands and fight like hellcats to get their way; they're slow to make love commitments, then so quick to break them; and they positively *attack* your body with intimidating insatiability. Hell, those sweet, helpless little dummies are dangerously cunning Delilahs!

Then again, maybe they're neither dummies nor Delilahs. Maybe our images are so at odds with each other because *neither* focuses on what women are really about. How can women be *both* too simple-minded to take seriously and too treacherous to trust? Maybe these images, too, make some women think that they're *supposed* to act these ways, whether they *feel* these ways or not. Of course, their script is too riddled with inconsistencies to create a coherent character. So they come off irrational, unpredictable, mysterious, wacky.

Take the contradictory stereotypes. Add them to woman's frustrating attempts to live up (or down) to both of them, then mix in all that spooky stuff that only females can do – menstruate, conceive, give birth, nurse – not to mention make you lose your heart. (Sounds like a witch's brew, doesn't it?) And it's easy to see why women are objects of your fear and loathing – and seem *so different*.

But let's look beyond the stereotypes. And let's separate women's acts from the facts and see what they're *really* like and how they're *really* different from you.

You're not going to get the radical feminist line from me that *all* the apparent differences are an act; that women are born with exactly the same abilities and personality proclivities as men and are simply held back from developing them. That's only a part of the story – one I won't bother to retell here. By now, we all know that girls are taught to be sugar and spice and everything nice and boys like nails and snails and puppy dog tails. And so people grow up into demure, diffident damsels and brave, boastful bullies. Yawn. That's too simple to be interesting or very accurate.

No, I think we'll find out that men and women are *innately* much more alike than they are different. But whatever genes sit on that X or Y chromosome tend to specialize them at certain talents and abilities, tit-for-tat. You're a little better at this. They're a little better at that. You think a bit more this way. They think a bit more that. Then Society tells us to be a *lot* more this or a *lot* more that and turns a few little cleavages into the Grand Canyon. But if we look at the Big Picture, even the Grand Canyon's just a little crack in the ground.

Anything You Can Do I Can Do Better

Let's begin with abilities. And let's get physical first.

It has nothing to do with sex-role learning that your woman comes running to you to open the mayonnaise jar, or cusses like a truck driver when she tries to unscrew the crankshaft. You're just plain *stronger* than she is, even if she's been pumping iron and swimming laps. Not that *all* men are stronger than *all* women, but most are stronger than most.

For starters, you're larger – all the better to hang more muscle on, take in more oxygen, and pump more blood. Your body's in fact *programmed* to make more muscle than hers, even with the same exercise (especially on your gorgeous chest and arms). Men also make better Tarzans because they physically mature more slowly and longer through their youth. So they keep building up hunkiness long after girls have acquired their curves. Since Mother Nature decided to sculpt these curves out of fat, the ideal young woman winds up with about equal proportions of fat and muscle (22 and 23 percent), while the ideal young you is 40 percent muscle and only 15 percent fat (add one more percentage point for each can of beer drunk per day). So don't tease her after you effortlessly open the mayonnaise.

There are other ways, though, that *women* are "tougher." *Because* of their fat, they have better endurance in long-distance sports. And in the game of survival (as opposed to football or hockey), they're the *stronger* sex. To begin with, they're more likely to be *born*, and born *normal* – not because they're more likely to be conceived (they're not), but because they're less vulnerable to prenatal problems and birth injuries. As life goes on, they're less susceptible to physical illnesses, too. So it's not just war and barroom brawls that make males die off quicker. This is why so many of you strong, virile men can wrestle a steer, challenge the Rockies, and lift Civics, but some cold microbes attack you and you topple like dead redwoods. CRASH into bed and depression.

In sexual response, the opposite sexes are a lot *less* opposite than we've been told. Remember hearing that women don't get turned on by erotic fantasies, pictures, and stories, like you do? Utter nonsense. Nancy Friday compiled books of women's sexual fantasies. And *trust* me that women get off reading them, along with *Penthouse* Forum and much of the very same stuff that you find head-throbbing.

Here's another misfounded myth: Women get turned on more slowly than men. You gotta massage 'em three minutes here, rub 'em five minutes there, get a little action going in between, and repeat the whole process with your tongue. Sort of like trying to start an old Model-T. Well, women were built for speed as well as comfort.

They can get an orgasm as fast as you can if they're masturbating. The reason why they enjoy, and need, so much foreplay with you is because they're *not* masturbating. They're getting off on *your* passionate presence, not their own fantasies (entirely), and on *your* tender touches, which, while deft, can't hit *all* the right places at all the right times. To climax, a woman needs the kind of African-rhythmic stimulation around her clitoris that a *hand* was made for – not your loin. It's as if you had to get off just on her squeezing your thighs. So since she's got a *technological* problem to deal with in intercourse, she's a longer time coming.

Of course, I don't have to tell you that women are just as sexual as you are. Probably some of you think that they're startlingly *more* sexual than men past their twenties. It's peculiar that it took all the hullabaloo about multiple orgasms to make us recognize that women are sexual at all. Homo sapiens have been around *how long*? And *this* was *news*?

Actually the Moslems knew it centuries ago. Unfortunately, the men were so terrified by their women's "implacable" passions that they instituted the custom of surgically removing clitorises. They would have been reassured by Masters and Johnson's findings. The bottom line is this: You just *can't generalize* about women. The vast majority are "orgasmic" (that's researchers' jargon for "hot"). And many of those often get off more than once. A few can keep firing like semi-automatic rifles (up to 50 times in one rendezvous with an electric vibrator). But women vary so much among themselves that you can't even compare them as a group to another group, say men.

Now, let's get cerebral and turn to matters of the mind.

How many women does it take to change a light bulb? About as many men as it takes to sew on a button.

The brain is the best place to see how egalitarian Mother Nature was when she "specialized" males and females at different skills, tit-for-tat. Mind you, the differences are minor. But there are quite a few of them. And when you add them all up into "general intelligence" and "creativity" measures, men and women don't differ overall *at all*.

A man's mind is made to perform better at: 1) visual-spatial tasks, which is why you find it easier than your woman to parallel park, follow football plays, and psyche out car engines; 2) physical manipulation, which is why she marvels at your fixing the toaster and shies away from "simple" mechanical tasks, like changing the oil; 3) math, at least the more advanced, spatial applications like analytic geometry and engineering, which is why she probably shined them on; and 4) fast-reaction tasks, which is why you avoid the potholes in the road she seems to aim for and why you see the double-play coming before she does.

Your male talents come in mighty handy in our high-tech world; in fact, your male talents *made* our world high-tech. Ironically enough, though, scientists speculate that your visual-spatial knack, quicker reaction time, and muscular physique evolved long, long ago to enhance your success at very *low*-tech skills like fighting and hunting. Apparently, Mother Nature figured that you fellas were more expendable than the gals back at the cave, since one ovum is worth a thousand sperm. Of course, she could have made more ova or more women or fewer sperm. But instead she made you eagle-eyed hunks.

The female faculties have a special flair for other tasks: 1) auditory memory, which is why your woman whimpers when you can't recall how "your favorite love song" goes (she can!); 2) tactile sensitivity, which is still a poor excuse for having her sew on your buttons and type your applications; 3) precision and detail, which is why she spells and punctuates better and uncannily remembers the date, time, place and circumstances of every first time you whatevered, and 4) verbal ability, which is why she can dash out longer and newsier messages, is less likely to stutter than a man, and may occasionally overwhelm you with her motor mouth.

In fact, it doesn't make much genetic sense that so few women have become great literaries, poets, and public speakers. From birth on, they've got the natural edge. They learn to speak, read, and write earlier. They were the goodie-two-shoes in school that made you slower, smart-ass boys look bad. Then later they do better at Scrabble, crossword puzzles, and even serious verbal creativity tests. Remember the sex differences in SAT scores in high school? Your verbal score put you in the top 30% of males, but only the top 40% of females. Of course, your math score looked positively Einsteinian in the female distribution.

One legendary female forte that does make genetic sense is "women's intuition." Let me explain. No doubt you've heard that even the least schizoid among us have a right brain and a left brain.

The right one thinks visually, spatially, synthetically, and in artistic and mechanical pictures and shapes. It drives for us, helps us change the spark plugs, and enjoys our trips to art museums. The left one thinks verbally, logically, analytically, and in words, numbers, and abstract symbols that don't look like what they really stand for. It deciphers insurance policies, balances our checkbook (sometimes), and fills out our tax forms.

In a baby and a young child, these brains work pretty tightly together – so much so that kids get left-brain reality confused with right-brain fantasy. Read them a monster story before bedtime and they might *see* monsters all night. But over time these brains get their acts less together. In fact, they physically separate. Since males take a little longer to mature, their brains have more time to pull apart and specialize. So men do a little better solving "specific" problems – the kinds that are either largely right brain (such as fixing the toaster or reading a map) or largely left brain (such as filling out the 1040 and following interest amortization tables).

Women, on the other hand, grow up more quickly, so their brains *specialize less* and *coordinate more*. You can't accuse their left brain of not knowing what the right brain is doing. Because there's such chatter going on between the two sides, women might seem confused doing the tasks you find so simple and understanding the processes you find so logical. ("But how will you know what fuse to change?" "How do you know which round thingy goes back on first when you change the washer?" "How can a plane push more air underneath it than it weighs?")

But what they *can* do better as a result is think "globally," "intuitively." They get the big, vague picture into focus. They *do* see the forest even if they miss a few trees. And since they're sensitive to detail, they miss precious few trees. At times, they're almost psychic. They look at photographs of an office party and can tell you who's loving and loathing who. (They're reading body language.) They "get a feeling" about whether your latest scam dream is going to work. (They're weighing not only its novelty and brilliance, but also its cost factors, its risk potential, and *your* managerial finesse with the grungy detail.) They "have a sense" of how you should dress for your visit to the I.R.S. office or the corporate boardroom, even if they've never been in one. (They grasp the subtle trappings of "class" and the subconscious "power" of different colors and styles.)

Maybe because women have this broad, fisheye view of the world, they score higher than men in social sensitivity and empathy tests. Show them a picture of a startled, worried woman opening the front door to a teenage boy and an older man, and they'll spin elaborate, right-on stories to make sense of the scene. Like it's her son and he's gotten in trouble with authorities. Or it's her husband who tracked down the youth who smashed her car. Show it to a man, and he'll puzzle over it a while before saying, "I guess she wasn't expecting them." A woman tends to pick up a lot more "delicate" social cues faster and then works with them more creatively.

She operates much the way you do on the highway using subtle *physical* cues to figure out where you are on a map – for example, the last junction you passed, traffic density, your odometer reading, the sun's location in the sky. If you don't think those cues are subtle, just get lost with an intelligent woman on your way to Chicago someday and see if you don't wind up in Miami.

Women's special savvy for psyching out social cues and situations develops very early. So it's not just a woman-made myth or a well-rehearsed line out of the sex-role script. Female infants clutching their pink blankets are more alert to their mommy's and daddy's facial expressions and tone of voice, and respond appropriately. Mommy is smiley and happy, Baby Sue giggles and coos. Junior might do anything, and he's probably more interested in pulling airplanes off his mobile.

Even female chimps show the social knack. They're famous for manipulating touchy situations to get what they want, usually using honey instead of vinegar. They don't just wait to be chosen by any old ranking male in the troop. They use their brains, butts, and bananas to *attract* their favorites and grunt "Not this year, honey" to the rest.

So when your woman tells you after a party, "I think the Morgans are having marital problems. Tom didn't look at Karen once after they walked in the door, and Karen was talking to that handsome young professor about going back to school...." – *believe her*. At least believe that she's onto something. You probably do in these cases. It's just when she says something about *your* interaction vis-à-vis her ("What's wrong? Why did you go off in a corner and talk with *her* all evening?") that you tend to get a bit defensive and discredit her social smarts.

Now, as I've been saying, these inherent sex differences, especially the ones above the neck, are *small*. Except on physical strength, the differences within the sexes are much greater than those *between*. "Sensitive" men have much more interpersonal savvy than the average women. And there are many women who do all the household budgeting, bill-paying, investing, and tax accounting with absolute wizardry. But Society takes *a few minor* differences and exaggerates them to the max – not always in the most efficient ways either.

Women *could* be applying their tactile sensitivity to auto mechanics and brain surgery, their precision to electro-chemistry and airline piloting, and their verbal ability to law and politics. But Society says "Think twice about traditionally male-dominated occupations. Even if you're good at math and like to play with mechanical things, you're a girl and not *supposed* to be good at those things. What you need is a good healthy dose of math anxiety. You'd better develop a way with words and a penchant for trivia so you can become an admin assistant or paralegal and rewrite reports and briefs for your boss."

Men *could* be using their physical strength for housework, their mechanical aptitude for the sewing machine, and their visual-spatial flair for crafting Christmas ornaments. But Society lays it on the line to them, too: "Perceptive about people and golden-tongued, are you? Then go out there and become a clever car salesman or corporate lawyer. Bend your spatial-mathematical leaning toward designing skyscrapers and bombs to flatten them with. Don't give away your gifts to anyone but the highest bidder, no matter how much you love home, children, flowers, and all that sentimental service stuff I extort out of women."

Society even creates some funny flip-flops. Women may have better honed verbal skills and a rep for being chatter-boxes and hen-heads. But according to fancy studies of conversational patterns, *men* talk *more* than women in sex-mixed groups. Women tend more to be asking the questions and men giving the answers. Men interrupt more, too, and women give in. This shouldn't be too surprising. Conversations are just mini-enactments of the sexual pecking order. Men are used to taking over and giving directives. Women learn to defer and shut up.

Is that the way things are meant to be? Well, let's look at personality differences between the sexes.

Why Can't a Woman Act More Like a Man?

Biologically speaking, there's very little preventing her, or preventing a man from acting more like a woman, for that matter. Psychologists have rigged up some pretty clever experiments to test out sex differences, and they haven't been able to find *any* consistent ones in dependency, sociability, nurturance, altruism, or – would you believe? – emotionality. In other words, contrary to our stereotypes, women are *by nature* no more giving (or selfish), needy (or independent), or irrational (or level-headed) than you men are on the average.

If you've seen otherwise, that doesn't mean you've been seeing things. Many women *seem* more giving because they're *asked* to give more. They have to deal more with the house and kids, plus be supportive to your career and community pursuits, even if they have their own going. In fact, from doll playing days on, they're told they're supposed to give or they'll never be able to catch and keep one of you.

Actually giving feels good. But only if you're getting back. And this is a real problem for women. Sometimes they give too much to everyone else, don't demand or get enough in return, and wind up with too little left over for themselves. It's the Classic Martyr Trip. Then, indeed, they start to *become* needy and dependent – and often hostile and whiney about how nobody appreciates all their suffering and self-denial. So if you take the rational approach and say, "Sweetheart, why don't you slow down and stop doing so much? Maybe we can hire somebody to help with the housework," you might get dumped on for being an ingrate. A woman, or anyone really, who's grown dependent won't snap out of it just by being given more independence. At least not until she just gets the appreciation she's knocking herself out for.

Women also *seem* to be more emotional because they express, while you repress. They've learned it's okay for them to display their feelings, especially the "softer" and so-called "weaker" ones that belie need and hurt. You've learned, on the other hand, that it's *not* so okay for you. Here's Society again carving out another chasm between the sexes and angling them into some pretty dastardly deals. It gives women a lot more expressive freedom, but both of you pay a price. They feel denied your expressiveness in return, and some of you *respect* them *less* for letting their hearts hang out, while you get ulcers and heart attacks holding yours in.

It all goes back to the language lesson in Chapter 1. Women say it with more emotion-packed punctuation. They "carry on forever." You "blow up" and quit. They ask for attention. You ask for sex. They refuse. You go off with the guys. But both of you are usually saying the same things: "Please reassure me." "Please understand me." "Please trust me." "Please do this one thing for me."

Another way that you're *not* different is how you approach problems. Myth has it that women are impulsive; they jump to unjam the toaster and make it worse. Well, they may. But another myth has it that they're just as likely to sit around helplessly till a man comes around. And they're probably *less* likely to kick the Coke machine than you are.

In fact, there's only one personality proclivity that seems to separate *most* of the boys from the *most* of the girls. And that's aggressiveness. Contrary to what you thought when you saw your woman and her mother go at it, *you men* are the true warriors of the species. You fight for play, for pride, for honor, for country, for money, and of course, for love. From boxing rings to boardrooms. From crap tables to courtrooms. From football fields to battlefields. From saloons to the stock exchange. You *love* a good fight. Even the most principled pacifists among you get off on electrozapping Space Invaders and smashing a softball. You quest to compete.

You're not only physically designed to fight; you're psychologically programmed to *want* to. Your "software" is the same hormone that also helps to hunk up your muscles: testosterone. It's loosely called "the male hormone" because once your body starts releasing large quantities of it around age 12 or 13 – well, *you* know what happens better than I do. But you have enough of it earlier to make you want to steal hubcaps, blow up frogs, and beat up the nerdy kid down the block. Girls and women have it pumping through their bodies, too, only less of it than most of you.

There have been all sorts of kinky experiments injecting the stuff into monkeys and mice to see what happens. The males, who already have plenty of it naturally, usually can't wait to pick a scruffy fight. When females get a shot before birth, they grow up to look a lot like males, to roughhouse like them, and even to master spatial tasks, such as running a maze, as well.

Scientists don't fool around with the stuff on people, but sometimes Mother Nature does. She's been known to make girls whose glands pumped too much testosterone in the uterus. And sure enough, just like the mice and the monkeys, they tended to look boyish, play tomboyish, and eschew the dating game.

Testosterone has a more subtle side than sparking fights and a more serious side than rousing roughhousing. Abetted by Society, it has helped create a "masculine ideal" that's very difficult to live up to and a male subculture that's very difficult to relax in. I feel for you men. You're always being tested, challenged, and sized-up – usually by one another. From the time you try to beat each other to the squeeze in a handshake, you're assessing: Who's got the greater athletic prowess? The sharper bargaining style? The better production team? The more sports knowledge? The sexier woman? The smarter investments? The bigger bank book? You're constantly jockeying for position. So you're always having to ask yourself, "How am I measuring up?" – whether against your worst enemy or your best friend.

The pressure's on just as heavily in *informal* social situations like cocktail parties and club picnics. At least at work there's an "official" pecking order. But at these "friendly fun" gatherings, you may not know whose hand you're gripping and your "status" rides on how you "perform" in brief, unpredictable encounters. You can wind up having the *worst* time, even if the beer was imported and the clam dip delectable, if you don't feel you scored well against the other men around. Your woman can't fathom why you're grumpy afterwards. You can't *bear* to talk about what's *really* gnawing at you. And when you give out a guarded hint or two, she either doesn't follow or can't genuinely understand.

It can be very lonely being a man.

American men probably have it the worst. Here it matters less than just about anywhere else what your father and grandfather did. You can't stand on their shoulders. Nobody's blood runs blue. You've got to achieve *for yourself,* *here* and *now.* If you've got a million bucks this week, you're a sharp dude. If you lose it next week, you're a dumb schmo. We also have a highly competitive survival-of-the-fittest ethic, one that shows little mercy for the meek, the mellow, and the maladapted. It all goes back to the Wild West wranglers and the early corporate Robber Barons. If you're one of those sensitive, liberated men seeking to get beyond it all, less stress and more power to you.

Of course, just because most women have less testosterone than most men doesn't mean they're *not* competitive. When they *have* to be, like in serious sports and business, they are as much so as men. And they're *far* more critical of each other's figures and faces as well as their own than men ever are. But they don't *challenge* each other on these things. They *never* say, "I bet I can get into this size 8 dress and you can't." In fact, they're more likely to say, "Gosh, I wish I had your tiny waistline (or slim hips or full tits)."

The fact that women don't go around challenging each other (or men) marks a real difference in style between the sexes. It's why so many women abhor war, weapons, fights, and violence. What "challenge" could be worth killing for? It's why they're do-gooders and would rather close gaps between people than dig them. It's why they don't bank their identities in abstract ideologies and opposing sides, and why they're suspicious of people (usually men) who do. Women don't trust the underlying "cockiness" – so aptly coined from a uniquely male feature. Maybe their lower self-confidence has something to do with it; some women are unsure of their abilities and resources. But I suspect that a little less testosterone makes them a little more humble and open-minded and a lot less interested in daring anyone to cross some line.

Women sometimes compete, *indirectly*, through *other* people, so the pressure's less on them. They don't talk much about it, but they know who's got the most successful/best looking/most attentive man and the cutest/smartest/nicest kids. Occasionally women compete for the same man, but rarely on the open field. It's usually when a man invites some Other Woman or two into the picture. And then the battle can rival Gettysburg.

Challenges to a woman's "territory" make compost of the notion that females are passive. They're about as passive as George Patton when it comes to protecting their *turf*, whether it be their home, children, job, reputation, or, especially, *their man*. They'll do almost anything for you. They're crazy about you. But notice, it's

How to Keep Your Woman

being on the *defensive* that brings out the tigress in them. You, by contrast, are more likely to get fired up *offensively* than they are.

Now you might very well be muttering "wait a minute," as you recall your last altercation with your woman. *She* was the one who "started it." *She* brought up the dirty socks scattered about the house, the leaky roof needing repair, the "communication problem" you didn't even know you had. *She's* always the one with the bitch, it seems. Isn't that taking the offense?

No, not quite. Recall again some of the idiomatic inversions in womanese. When *she's* not feeling quite right about *you*, she may project that *you're* not feeling quite right about *her*. Why? Because she doesn't feel *powerful* enough inside to confront her own true feelings and then confront you with them.

Well, bitchiness flares up out of a sense of powerlessness, too. At some point in the past, she may have matter-of-factly asked you to pick up your socks, fix the roof, or talk about the funk you were in. You probably saw her point and maybe even promised to do so. But you keep forgetting about your socks (they're not of life-and-death importance). You plan to fix the roof in the next few weekends, but not in the next half-an-hour (as she has in mind). And sometimes part of your funk is simply not wanting to talk about it.

In any case, she feels that her sweet, calm requests were ineffectual. They failed to inspire your attention and action. She may even suspect that you're *purposely* subverting her wishes to get back at her for something or to prove you're not pussy-whipped. And you may suspect that the dirty socks or the leaky roof isn't the "real issue," though it usually is. So she feels frustrated, impotent, pissed, maybe even hurt. She also feels put on the defensive wondering why you seemingly ignored her. Your non-action may look like an offensive move to her. At the same time, she makes a *rational* decision to drop the first "unsuccessful" strategy to motivate you and try a new one.

Under the heat of her emotions, though, the tactics she cooks up can be a bitch's brew. She may get angry and run you down (but rarely any lower than how *she's* feeling). She may whimper and try to guilt-trip you. She may wildcat-strike come dinner or bedtime in the hopes of forcing a collective bargain.

At this point, *you* start to get frustrated. You're thinking, "Why doesn't she use a carrot instead of hitting me over the head with a stick?" Well, what she's *intending* to do is *hit* you with a *carrot* – the carrot being that she'll *stop* bitching, whimpering, or withholding as soon as *you* do what she's been asking you to do. Of course, a fresh carrot stings as sharply as a stick. So you can't be blamed for missing the difference.

But if you realize where *she's* coming from – the defensive line on a losing team – you should feel less under attack. And you might even be able to break through her defense. If you tell her that you *understand* her hurt and angry feelings, they'll magically start to dissolve. Then if you make a noticeable effort to fulfill her requests even *halfway* (pick up *some* socks, *schedule* the roof-fixing, tell her your boss's *ties* depress you, anything), you may never hear them again. Women aren't *that* demanding. They just can't stand to feel *ignored*. Who can?

There's another brand of bitchiness that festers on yet another type of powerlessness. She wants to be "the Great Woman behind the Great Man." But instead she comes off like "the Pushy Woman driving her Good Man to an early grave." She wants you to be more ambitious, more successful, and make more money so you both can have a nicer house, a better car, a bigger this, and a finer that. Typically, the woman who slips into this syndrome feels a lot more miserable about *her own* lack of success than you do having to listen to her. The problem – no, *her* problem – is that she committed herself to you believing, justifiably or not, that *you'd* reach a certain status that *she* wanted to reach by now, and she tied *her* aspirations to *you*. Maybe you led her on; maybe you didn't. That's not as relevant as the fact that she made herself *dependent* upon *you* to realize a dream of *hers*. Maybe you encouraged that dependency; maybe you didn't. What matters *now* is that she's suffering from an acute lack of power to realize her own dream. She gave you that power, and you're stuck with her frustration.

This may be one of the dearest debts that we all – men and women – have to pay for sexual inequality. As long as an ambitious woman isn't encouraged or appropriately rewarded to set the world on fire for *herself,* some *man* will be prodded to do it for her. It's a sorry set-up for both sexes. Even if a man *does* hit it rich and buys his woman's happiness, does that accrue into *love*? Probably not; the currencies don't exchange.

Why Men Write the Songs

What songs? The *love* songs, of course. Most of the songs ever written are love songs. Love longed for. Love chanced. Love found. Love shaken. Love deceived. Love lost. Love embittered. Then love longed for again. And most of the continuing drama is composed by you men. Certainly the economic pressures on you have a lot to do with your passionate productivity. But so does your raging, unrelenting romanticism, or you'd sing about football and firearms. (The other thing you make music about is war, which is what inspired marches and some national anthems.)

So let's look at why you're the romantics of the species – why you fall in love more rapidly and out of it more slowly than women tend to.

1. *Men Are Mama's Boys*. Let's start with the farthest-out explanation, the psychoanalytic *á la Freud*. It contends that little boys develop a much stronger initial love for Mommy than for Daddy, so they grow up to be deeply dependent on women. (Just ask Oedipus.) Little girls, on the other hand, form equally rich attachments with both parents – with Mommy because...well, she's *Mommy*, and with Daddy because...well, he's the only hunk around. So before they mature into women, they've spread their risk. They're not so dependent upon men alone, so they're more cautious when wooed, less tolerant when disappointed, and more resilient when left on their own.

Well, maybe.

2. *Women Survey the Heart Land*. Then there's the biologically-based theory that, since women are more attuned to the social and emotional lay of the land, they're more sensitive to the ridges and gullies in their own love relationships. They're more likely to explore exactly how they feel *now*, and contrast it with how they've felt in the past and how they could feel under the best of circumstances. (They have a little computer whirring in their heart, too.) It's true that the more rocks you turn over, the more likely you're going to find a rattlesnake. But at least you know what's out there.

You men, on the other hand, are *homesteaders*. You're happy just to share common ground with your woman to settle down on. The idea of a stable institution like marriage is more *sacred* to you than to women. In fact, just about all institutions are. You've been known to lay down your life for your country, your form of government, your religion, your economy, and your law. Most institutions were *invented* by men, including, it's suspected, marriage (so you could know which kids were yours). Not that women laugh them off like late-night board games. But they are more concerned about the emotional impact on the players. This is another reason why they don't like war and survival-of-the-fittest set-ups. By the same token, if they're not having a good time playing Marriage, they want to either change the rules or set a time limit.

To take the theory one step further, women may learn to manage and control their emotions better than men do. True, they may *express* them more freely. But once the tear ducts run dry and the anger burns out, they're purged of the poison. They're ready for the practical business of regenerating more appropriate, productive attachments – like to their work, their children, their friends, and other men.

This reasoning runs pretty true to experience. But it does overlook the fact that women also overturn rocks in search of the rare and wonderful wild flowers of a relationship. The rattlesnakes they happen upon bite like hell. And sucking out the venom is a pretty unsavory process.

3. *Men Can Afford to Love for Love*. Think back when you were scouting around for a woman to love – *really love* and call your own. What was important to you? She had to have a nice personality, look attractive (at least to you), be reasonably intelligent, and share enough values and dreams with you, right? All that was important was her *as a person*. You didn't particularly care about what her daddy did, or what she did, or how much she made, or who her broker was. You wanted to know what made her laugh, what turned her on, and what she did for fun.

After you met this Special Person, it didn't take you long to realize you'd struck gold. You got to know what you needed to know pretty quickly in the process of spending a few enchanted evenings together. In fact, you really didn't know a whole lot of hard facts about her before you let yourself go and took the lover's leap.

Men fall in love so *exquisitely*, so *beautifully*, so *totally*. What they don't know about their woman, they assume the best. When it isn't, they give her every benefit of the doubt. She can do no wrong. She can walk on water. She's everything a man could ever want.

Sigh! If only woman could afford the luxury of this pure, romantic love for a man. Unfortunately, *they can't*. Unless they're independently bankrolled, their social and economic rung in life is largely (though not totally) dependent upon their man's, since men usually get boosted up the ladder faster. When they choose a man, they're not only picking a personality, face, and soul-mate; they're settling on a *standard of living*, a whole life style, and a set of opportunities for their children.

So, it takes women longer to let go and love. They have more research to do. They *are* interested in what your daddy does, what you do, what you make, and who your broker is. They're watching to see how effectively you work, how ambitious you are, how well you get along with your coworkers, how "steady" you're likely to be. Sounds like a job interview, doesn't it? Well, it sort of is one. You play suitor; she plays recruiter. And a very careful one, since you're often talking about life-long fulltime employment.

Women are funny. They often shy away the "dirty" bargaining business of stock exchanges, labor unions, and backroom politics. But they take a tough, pragmatic approach to cutting the best possible deal on the marriage market. Some are no more romantic about it than you are negotiating for a used car, and a few get damn mercenary about it. It's true, I'm afraid. Some women still marry mostly for money. (Quite a few have freely, even laughingly, admitted it to me.) In particular, wives of doctors, lawyers, and hell-bent businessmen. "Why not?" they tell me. "I knew he'd be too busy at work and too burned out afterwards to make love or conversation. I traded off companionship for my Cadillac, cashmere, and country club."

Not that all or even *most* women prefer an afternoon shopping spree at Saks to an evening love fest with a man. Not many put their hearts on hold just to wait for Mr. Millionaire. There are, of course, a lot of women who'd like to find him, but doubt they have the social and physical bait to bag him. Still, plenty value your good company and affection right up there with bucks and ambition, if not higher. They may feel they're playing a price, though – one that you don't have to – for indulging their romantic fancies: They're trading off financial fancies, or working themselves to fill in the shortfall.

What all this means for you in the long-term is that the more materialistic woman may be *easier* to keep, *as long as* you keep bringing home the material. Unless her priorities change over time, she's not likely to demand much of your time, libido, and tenderness. The more romantic woman, though, *will*. After all, she "paid" for them. If she senses you're faltering, she'll feel cheated in the deal. Can you blame her?

Bridging the Gender Gap

Biologically speaking, men and women *can't* be *too* far apart. We're each fashioned from 46 chromosomes – 23 from Mom and 23 from Dad – and only *one* of them (from Dad) has anything to do with our sex. That's not much room to differ. It can only call a few of the shots that make us into what we become. Forty-five others are calling the rest.

The sex differences that result aren't very large, and they complement each other nicely. While you're fixing the carburetor, she can hum that neat tune you can't remember and tell you what "really happened" at the party last night. After you play a computer game and she finishes her emails to friends and family, you can give her pointers at chess. Then you can slip off together to make love. You see, if you can both accept and respect whatever little differences *do* exist, your love can flow *through* them instead of around them. You can fill in one another's blanks and can each feel you've found your Other Half.

The gaps that draw battle lines are typically the ones that Society carves. From tot-hood on, it raises girls and boys in separate, almost antagonist worlds – you in one spiked with toy guns and tests of toughness, and her in one laced with tiny tea sets and the discipline of daintiness. You grow up in a pee wee war zone, she in a dollhouse of detention. As you mature, Society sticks you with too many challenges and responsibilities, and her with too little life control and confidence. It breeds male meanness and repression against female frustration and fear.

Then Society sends you, and usually your woman too, off to joyless jobs, or may lock up one of you with the kids all day. Either way, you're both drained at night and needy for nurturance. But who's got it to *give*, and how do you *get* it? You don't feel free to show you're needy, so she feels shut out. She *does* feel free to show she's needy, but then you feel put upon.

And so the battle of the sexes rages – flares of frustration followed by cold-war isolation. Understanding is unable to slip behind the lines. You each have your side: both valid, both threatened. So neither side dares lay down your arms.

Well, there's no stronger unifying force than a common enemy. So why don't you both join forces and gang up on the hawk that started it all? That's right – *Society*. But guess who Society is? That's right – we have met the enemy and it is *us*. It is all of us who push any part of Macho Manhood and Wimpy Womanhood on ourselves and our children. All of us who shun opportunities to merge our worlds. All of us who don't bother to understand the other sex. All of us who won't drop the act surrounding our own gender roles.

You see, becoming a peacemaker in the battle of the sexes isn't so much a matter of *laying down* your arms as it is opening them.

Chapter 4.

Keeping Her vs. Keeping Her the Way You Love Her: What Do You Want to Keep in Your Woman?

"How do I love thee? Let me count the ways?" When was the last time you counted the ways you love your woman? You know, the things you love and appreciate about her. Why bother? Because *conscious* gratitude and appreciation will probably leak out into your behavior towards her. You'll treat her better. Then you'll be much more likely to keep her as well as keep her the way you love her. If you just take her virtues for granted, you'll turn into a lazy lover and delude yourself into thinking that the sweet spot you're in with her now will never sour. And you might not even notice the signs that she's slipping away from you by either leaving you or going to seed.

So think back and take stock: Why did you fall in love with your woman to begin with? Why *her*? Why not any of the other gals you ran with? I know this isn't easy for you. Men often have a tough time reconstructing those blurry early days of night-long intimate talks, flashes of uncontrollable passion, and poetry pouring out of their mouth. Even if you do remember, you may hit the wall trying to put into words exactly what bait hooked you.

Having trouble? Let me jog your memory by giving you some typical reasons why men get caught in a woman's silky web.

1. She's beautiful.

For a man, this is the most basic reason of them all. Initially, you go for the prettiest piece of candy in the bowl and just hope it will taste good. Why get to know her if she's not a fox? This is why a woman's beauty makes a bigger difference than her brain in how far up the socio-economic ladder she marries. This is why Helen of Troy's face launched a thousand ships. This is why Mark Antony ended his life. You don't see men going into battle and losing their kingdoms over Ugly Betty or the Golden Girls.

You men are realistic, however. When you picked out your woman, you were looking for the prettiest candy in *your* bowl – not George Clooney's or Brad Pitt's. You know that their potential selections are considerably classier than yours. (They are also higher maintenance.) But in the case of your woman, she was the sweetest fruit in *your* orchard, even a bit juicier than what you figured you'd harvest.

Some of your woman's beauty is in her eyes and her smile – the way she looks at you when you've done something *really right* by her, like when you've made her proud, touched her heart, or turned her on. Then she gives you that warm, embracing look that melts the core of you. You'll do almost anything to get that look – except take out the garbage or pick up your socks without her telling you three times. Try doing these tasks the first time she asks you or *without* her asking you at all. You might just get that look from her. (If not *that* look, the look of utter shock.)

Beyond that look, what you consider beautiful is a matter of personal taste, of course. For some men, it's blonde hair and blue eyes. For others, bronze skin and brown hair. For some, a thin, athletic body. For others, some tender meat on the bones. Some of you are "tit men" who go for voluptuous breasts you can sink your lips into. Or you may count yourself among the "ass men" who are seeking the well rounded, jelly-tight butt. Thank God, there's a cover for every kettle!

If you had your druthers, you'd stop your woman's clock so she could forever look exactly the way she did the day you fell in love with her. Short of that fat chance, the next best thing you can do is to continue to appreciate her good looks and *tell her that you do*. She'll consciously do her part to try to delay the signs of decay, and you'll unconsciously do yours by overlooking them and always finding her beautiful.

2. She's sexy.

Of course, you may think your woman is sexy because of her great body parts or her tight, athletic build. Or maybe you're captivated by her long, flowing hair. When you first saw her, those were the things that caught your eye. But after you get to know a woman, other features about her take center stage.

You've probably heard that the major sex organ in the body is the brain. Maybe the main reason you find her so sexy is because she looks at you like she *wants* you. And this is what you want to keep most in your woman – her desire for *you*, specifically her desire to have *sex* with you. Nothing turns you on like her desire. Conversely, nothing turns you off like a woman's sexual indifference towards you.

Ask her what she finds sexy about you. Don't assume you know because women's tastes are as varied as the ways they achieve orgasm. Some women like a tight butt. Others love a big chest and shoulders; they make her feel secure and protected. Almost none like a beer belly, however you may have acquired it. Some are attracted to a lot of hair on your head, and others prefer none. But if she's really being honest and comprehensive, she'll tell you it's something in your personality, like the way you make her laugh. She may even cite your character, which may not sound sexy at all, but it is. Many women love a man who stands for something, who has impeccable integrity, who has a bigger-than-both-of-you cause to live for. On the other hand, material girls are turned on by whatever in you brings in the big bucks. That could be your ambition, cleverness, ruthlessness, dominance, greed, quest for power, or some other Alpha-dog trait. Call it anti-character or whatever you like, but it's something inside you, not a body part.

Chances are she *won't* tell you she finds your "big dick" sexy. First of all, size is overrated; it all depends on *her* size and how you *fit*. Secondly, women find dicks – well, not particularly attractive in themselves – at least not to look at. Oh, she may have developed a good relationship with yours and even given it a name, but that's to make it more – shall we say, palatable?

Whatever your woman finds sexy about you, stay like that or keep doing it. In turn, she'll stay the sexy way you love her.

3. She's adventurous.

Due to their lower testosterone level, women are innately more cautious than men. If they weren't – if they all gleefully went off to war, raced anything with wheels, surfed in a hurricane, and went hunting with Dick Cheney – our species never would have survived this long. So you're particularly impressed when your woman will walk on the wild side. Of course, your idea of wild might not be the next guy's. For the wives of "Deliverance" rednecks, shopping in a town of more than ten thousand is pretty risky behavior. If you dabble in extreme sports like skateboarding and freestyle motocross, she might have to bungee jump or skydive to gain your respect.

For some of you, it's important that she's willing to try new things in bed – dress up like a Catholic schoolgirl, prance around in spike heels, don some leather, wear a mask, get spanked, spank you – hey, all kinds of crazy things go on between consenting adults. In fact, she may be the one to initiate the fantasy, which will either bond you to her forever or scare the hell out of you.

But your definition of adventure may run beyond the bedroom. Maybe you like the fact that your woman loves to travel, or go out on the boat, or ride on the back of your motorcycle. Maybe she experiments with preparing unusual dishes or making up her own – and they work. Maybe she raises snakes, rock climbs, scuba dives, hikes, or even grows orchids, which isn't dangerous but sure is easy to fail at. Whatever it may be, she does something that makes you proud and may even make your testosterone flow.

4. She has a great sense of humor.

Hopefully, this means more to you than the fact that she laughs at your jokes. Of course, you do want her to keep laughing at your jokes and smiling through your stories, even when she's hearing them for the tenth time, right? But more generally, one of things you so liked about your woman early on was how she rolled with life's little punches. She knew how to make the best of things, how to make lemonade out of lemons, and how to laugh off her own follies and foibles.

Most important to you, she knows how to laugh off *your* follies and foibles. Imagine what your life would like if she didn't, if she put you down every time you forgot to pick up milk at the grocery store, or had a little too much to drink, or choked the garbage disposal. Maybe you're a little older and pursuing more fateful follies, like a big-hog Harley or sleek little sports car you can't really afford, or a serious flirtation with a younger woman you can't afford either. When you come to your senses, you'd like your woman to make light of your boyish misbehavior, wouldn't you. Her showing a sense of humor when you screw up is her form of forgiveness.

5. She respects you.

     A woman shows you respect in a million little ways. By not kicking you out of the house when you let out a noisy fart and LOL. By smiling in silence when you boast about triumphs and conquests that she knows you didn't quite achieve. By not interrupting you while you're telling friends a story that you've stretched into a tall tale. In fact, a woman most often shows respect for her man by not sharing her true thoughts when he's done something mildly stupid. This is something you want your woman to keep doing, don't you.

     If your woman respects you, she's probably doing other things that you never see – like defending you when her mother makes an unsavory remark about you, or letting her friends and family know when you've completed a major task or accomplished a goal or have finally been rewarded for your hard work and intelligence. If she's happy about something you've done, you can bet she'll be telling everyone she knows.

6. She's a Madonna.

     Not the singer, guys. I'm talking about the sacred, not the profane. I mean you think of your woman as pure, chaste, virginal, and undefiled by the likes of you. You perch her high on a pedestal, if not an altar, and practically worship her. Sure you have sex, but you handle her like a goddess rather than a whore. The whole operation is somehow "clean," unsoiled, uncontaminated.

     The problem is that, when you madonnasize a woman, you may not want to try kinky combos and exploits with her, nor do you want her to initiate them either. (If she would be *willing*, however, she's all the more saintly in your eyes!) Worse yet, you may stray in search of a woman who'll play the whore with you. After all, a lot of men need a whore in their lives. They just don't want to be committed to one or have children with her. They just want to unleash their libido on one, acting out their darkest fantasies. The male urge to love and cherish a Madonna while sharing passion and porn with a whore no doubt gave rise to the system of wives and concubines in ancient Rome, China, and the Middle East (check out the *Old*

Testament) and later, the idealized wife-plus-mistress arrangement in Europe and Latin America.

Those times have pretty much passed, save for very wealthy. Now you have to choose between grace and sin, so to speak. If you love your woman for her virtue, wholesomeness, and goodness, you've taken the hallowed high road and want her to preserve those angelic qualities.

7. She's smart.

Used to be that a man wanted a woman to be dumber that he was. So he wound up with either a dull, helpless woman who had to depend on him to do everything – that was fun, wasn't it – or a very bright woman, probably brighter than he was, who knew how to act dumb during the courtship phase. After she won his heart, she dropped the act and let him know who was boss. That was fun, too, huh.

In the past few decades, you men discovered that having an intelligent partner is lot easier and more entertaining than having a dim-witted one. She is less likely to make major mistakes managing money, her career, the kids, and the house, and she is better able to help you with traditional male tasks as well, like fixing things or getting them fixed, choosing among insurance and financial options, and even maintaining the cars. In addition, she's more fun to be with. Your conversations sparkle and last longer. You share more interests. You learn from each other. You try on one another's viewpoints. You stimulate each other's thinking. You get each other's jokes and laugh together more. You inspire each other to be better persons. This is *way* better than the traditional power imbalance and struggle.

Both men and women made this quiet revolution possible. Once women acquired a sense of their own high value and recognized how society had denied it, they took off like rockets. What disadvantaged group has risen so rapidly through the occupational structure? Medicine, law, academia, politics, architecture, aviation, even engineering boast significant numbers of competent women. Women are now completing more education than men – and performing better in almost all subjects. If you're prehistoric enough to prefer a dumb woman, you'll have a tough time finding very many.

Thankfully, few of you men think this way anymore. While women were growing more confident, so were most of you. You feel more comfortable around a woman because, at last, you can be you! You can make mistakes, change your mind, apologize, and do all those wonderful non-macho things that men thought they couldn't do years ago when they had to put up a hard front. Now *those* men were insecure and couldn't tolerate challenge from their women. But these days you're at home with and up to the challenge. So we can all be ourselves.

Anything else you want to keep in your woman? Maybe you love the way she decorates the house or dresses up or clips coupons. Maybe you love her cooking, her CD collection, or her accent. Add them to the list, no matter how small. These are things that will motivate you to do whatever you must to keep her and to keep her from going the seed, which is the unpleasant botanical topic of the next chapter.

Chapter 5.

How to Tell She's Going to Seed – Before It's Too Late

If you've ever been a backyard fruit and veggie gardener, you know what "going to seed" is all about. It means you left that godzilla-sized zucchini on the vine too long. While you were watching exposition football, its seeds beat you to the pick-off and turned your squash into squish.

When a woman goes to seed, the result is unfortunately much the same. She loses her sensual succulence, her witty crispness, her spontaneous sweetness, her physical firmness. She's no longer quite the way you love her, not quite the same woman you fell in love with. If you found her under a leaf today, you might not pick her at all.

A man *knows* if it's happened to his woman – so does everyone else – and it's the most romantically disillusioning experience of his life just to face the fact head-on. To gaze at her naked body in bed and admit it leaves him limp, or repelled. To realize how long it's been since they really "connected" in meaningful talk, run-away laughter, or alluring glances. To concede that he's no longer proud to be seen with her, that she's a detracting social object at his side. Then to deal with his guilt over feeling this way, while juggling his resentment, his pain, his despair, and his fantasies to find romance elsewhere. Plus to control that ego-eating fear that maybe he's no longer virile and attractive and is simply getting what he deserves.

Well, take heart, dear Gentlemen. *Veggies* were meant to go to seed. *Fruit* were meant to go to seed. But *women aren't*. If women were, they'd go to seed the same way fruit and veggies do – if they *aren't picked*. The way women usually go to seed, which is *after* they've been picked – totally defies all natural law.

Now don't go running to your women citing this chapter and verse and make us *both* an enemy. This view isn't very popular with women, especially those who are drooping on the vine. I tried it out on a seed-smart Earth Mother I interviewed – one prematurely past harvest time – and she called me a "hot-house misogynist." (That's no tomato; it's a woman-hater). She went on to try to "correct my karma" with a "more liberating" law of nature: *All* living things are designed to "degenerate" after making the seeds of the next generation. Ergo, women "naturally" get plain and portly during their childbearing years. "But what about men?" I ventured to ask. "Don't they make seeds, too, and stay trim and terrific-looking?" "Not really, "she scowled, "they're only the fertilizer."

The fact is, though, Mother Nature doesn't leave women to rot in the dirt after dropping a couple of kids, and I'll take Mother Nature's laws over Earth Mother's any day.

What Sets Off the Going-to-Seed Syndrome

Nonetheless, there are some natural processes and some *not-so-natural* ones – man-made and woman-made – that make it hard for a woman to stay in bloom.

The War Against Weight. Just as Mother Nature made you to amass muscle, she made women to amass *fat*. The stuff makes up 36% of the average American woman vs. only 26% of the average American you. Every extra atom of food they eat gets hooked onto a fat molecule. That's why prideful women are on diets all the time. It's why they've evolved a mystical dietary cosmology to explain how just their *looking* at a chocolate sundae adds weight. It's why they'll trade you half their dinner for a bird-size bite of yours and hide their rice under the watercress. Even if they're active, their miles-per-meal is high, and, unlike your car, it gets higher over the years.

Believe me, it's a bitch. That's why it takes a very attentive, appreciative man to make it worth battling the bulge for. But, believe me, for *that* kind of man, women can move mountains of food away.

The battle is downright brutish after a baby because there's not only new fat to fight; there's new *flab* to firm. Women who have never tried or stuck with an exercise program before – and that makes up the majority – may retreat in terror from a regimen and surrender to a flabby fate. Why kill yourself, some figure, when there're so many *other* women around who've lost *their* war against weight and haven't lost their *man*?

Of course, going to seed involves more – *a lot* more – than succumbing to sweets and spaghetti. A woman's very *personality* changes. She becomes less lively, less responsive, less sexual, less…well, *interesting to be with*, at least with her man. She can get downright dull or, worse yet, turn sour.

For humans, going to seed is ultimately a *psychological* syndrome (which it isn't for fruit and veggies). It's a woman's subconscious *choice* to let go, give up, and run down. But *why*? Let's look at the categories of seeders I've seen. Bear in mind that these are "pure strains" and many actual cases are "hybrids."

Post-Wedding Poop Out. Some women have to try harder than others to score on the marriage market. Or at least *they* feel they do. Maybe they're not naturally beautiful, cute, or sexy, or slim, shapely, and taut. Or they have one kind of personality that Portnoy complained about. Or they're too shy or retiring or airy upstairs to make sparkling conversation. Or even when they try very hard, all they can manage is drivel about Aunt Emma's gallstones and the world's best dishwasher. Their fondest hobby may be couponclipping and their major interest, movie star romances.

What these women have is a "marketing" problem, and they put forth herculean effort trying to look good and act charming so they can find a man.

The problem is that they get *tired*, sometimes even bitterly so. Often they're innately low-energy and not particularly intimacyoriented. But they're eager to get married and do the house-and-babies routine, in addition to whatever they do outside the house. Since they usually know their weaknesses, they'll typically let courtship conversation revolve around their man because it builds his ego and makes them *seem* charming. But attentively gazing into his eyes while making mental lists of wedding guests turns into an exhausting act. So does adopting all his tastes, interests, and opinions, if only for a while. And so does counting every calorie, keeping up a snazzy hairstyle, and reconstructing a new face every morning – especially when she's doing it *for a him* instead of for *herself.*

When the wedding day comes, she's crying tears of relief. Thank God, she thinks, she can finally let down and lay back! Ah, planted at last! So naturally enough, she starts to go to seed by the end of the season.

But most women take longer.

Security Slippage. At some point, maybe after so many anniversaries or babies, some women get to feeling a little *too rooted, too secure* in the relationship, *too comfy* with their man. He's been so steady – home for dinner every night – and so sweet – helpful with the dishes and diapers – and so tolerant – unflappable fixing the garbage disposal for the fifth time. For all he's enjoyed and endured, he's not about to leave. He wouldn't *think* of leaving. Hell, he's soaked so much time, money, and obligation into this set-up that he's too invested to leave! Besides, he's too big a sweetheart.

And so a woman may grow a tad lazy. She may start to lean more heavily on her man's sense of duty and humor, and less so on herself to keep *attracting* him back to the hearth. So she may start to slip here and there and eventually let herself go entirely.

You've no doubt heard of a *man* taking a *woman* for granted. (Maybe you've been accused of the crime yourself.) It usually means he's not giving her the time, affection, or appreciation that he *once* did and that she feels she needs and deserves. Well, Security Slippage is the most common version of a *woman* taking a *man* for granted. Either way, for the "Taken," it's the Devil's reward for being good.

When a man does the taking, though, his woman is his *only* victim. He abuses her or ignores her, but he seldom takes his indifference out on *himself.* So she feels free to call foul. But when a *woman* does it to her *man*, she often abuses and ignores *herself* in the process. So he's in a bind. It seems macho-mean to get angry and call her on taking *you* for granted when she's taking *herself* for granted as well. It seems much more gentlemanly to quietly tend to duty and let your love turn to pity. Sigh.

Living-the-Dream Letdown. Here is the case of the basically happy, traditional woman who has done everything she was "supposed to" do by her early thirties – finish school, start a nice career, marry a nice man, move into a nice house, and have a couple of nice, normal babies. She's *not* disappointed. In fact, she's *delighted.* She has *all* she ever wanted. But there's nothing *left* to quest for and accomplish. Nothing to put real *energy* into. So, plop – she's as good as in the ground.

There *is* plenty to *do*, however – all kinds of daily dictates to keep her busy: changing diapers, washing out bottles, entertaining toddlers, doing laundry, shopping, fixing meals, and keeping her dream house spic 'n span. She's a damn good housewife and mother, and may even be working, too. But she does all her activities on an as-it-comes-up basis. It's *maintenance*, not mission; just "keeping up," not questing.

And guess who tends to get the *least* maintenance: *her man.* Why? Because he makes the fewest day-to-day demands. He's the wheel that squeaks the least, so he's the last to get the grease. After all, he washes, dresses, and feeds himself and never needs ironing. So she puts the relationship on hold for a while, sometimes a *long* while. Intimacy yields to domesticity. Romance falls by the wayside.

Of course, he's not the only one lost in the shuffle. She loses *herself* in it, too. To her, the shuffle is *all* that's left to do. And it doesn't demand she look stunning and sexy. It doesn't require or inspire her to be fun and exciting. And so those cherished charms get put away like fine china and silver. She brings out only her practical virtues for everyday use.

Biting-the-Bullet Blues. This woman, too, has done everything she was "supposed to do" early in life – get educated, marry, buy the house, have the kids. But she *is* disappointed – in the extreme, living a nightmare. She feels *stuck* in the ground, like she's dying on the vine, with nothing to keep her from going to rot. She's the most common of all seeders I've seen, and prevention or cure requires testing her soil to find out what's killing her.

Maybe she has all she ever thought she wanted, but she's left wondering, "Is this *all* there is?" Maybe she settled for *less* than she wanted in a man or his money and regrets the deal. Or maybe she thought he was right at the time, but he turned out to be *all wrong*. Maybe he *was* right and potentially *is*, but he's too busy or distracted to give her what she needs. Maybe the hubby-house-and-babies routine was never really her cup of tea, but it was the only one poured in her head. Or maybe it just can't compare to her early peaks as Homecoming Queen, valedictorian, or the lead in the school play. Whatever it is that's eating at her, its bite is poisonous.

Still, she has her reasons to stay around and stick it out. She may be scared to venture away. She may not know anything else better to do or whether she can do it. She may even be too depressed to build dreams. Or her religious beliefs may constrain her. Or the till-death-do-us-part ideal does. Or she can't get past "what people will think." Or the children. Or finances. Or her fear that she's gone so far to seed that she'd never be marketable again.

Sometimes the Blues turns bitter and bitchy. But it can go underground, too – like one case I witnessed. The couple started out a fair, fun-loving match. But pretty soon she wanted to build a nest and have babies while he wanted to step up their pace to faster-lane living. So she went to work for her dream house, while he went back to school. She sneaked in a couple of "accidents" over the years, but only in between the abortions he insisted upon. As she got more of her way, he went more his own.

She went to seed fast. She chopped off her locks, gained 30 pounds, dressed like a school marm, and lost interest in sex. As she narrowed her after-work orbit to the kids and television, leaving him well out of range, he broadened his world and added a lover, which she pretended not to see. When he'd gently threaten to leave, she'd sincerely promise to reform, then lose five pounds but gain back ten.

Yet, barely a cross word e'er passed their lips. Maybe she didn't know it – certainly she'd never *admit* it – but she grew to *hate* her guy's guts. She repressed her resentment and used her own sagging self as a weapon of revenge. (Why didn't *he* leave? Pity, guilt, duty, money, habit. But he ran these reasons eventually and did leave.)

Empty Nest Emptiness. Finally, there's a small but especially sad class of women who fade out on the home stretch. They lived the traditional dream. Without wondering too hard what they might have been – they've never had a serious career – they helped make their husband, kids, and home all *they* could be. But now their man is peaking out and looking toward retirement. Their kids are striking out and looking toward graduation, career, marriage, and family. Their home is quiet, kempt – too much so for comfort – and ready to go on the housing market. Their marriage has respectfully rutted. So what's there left to live for?

Maybe lots in theory. But that's not where these women are coming from. They've lived a day-to-day existence, and they're left with no tomorrow. Besides, it takes a lot of energy to build a new routine – to learn to paint, to join a club, to plan a trip, to even find out what you *like*. These women may not have the voltage left to light up their own lives. They've given so much to others over so many years. They may have forgotten how to give to *themselves*, if they ever knew.

Unless they get a new act together, they tend to fill up their idleness with little self-destructions: eating, gossiping, watching all the soaps, washing already clean floors, withdrawing and weeping at times, chatting endlessly at others, meddling in their children's affairs, and sometimes sneaking booze and stimulants.

As bad as the Empties are in themselves, these women can make their situation worse. Kids resent Mom's intrusions and find her dependency "sick." They can ruthlessly push her away in disgust when she's needy to make herself needed. A husband, too, may not be there on call. There's a chance he'll die off of a coronary or cancer and leave her to drown in bills and legalities. There's also the chance that he'll *leave*. It's not uncommon these days for the middle-aged man to branch out and discover the world he's been missing. Along the way, he may just find some lively young woman in her thirties or forties who shares the view of his new horizons. If his wife isn't up to the challenge, she may just be left to wither alone.

The Stages of Going to Seed

It doesn't happen overnight and it isn't irreversible. But the warning signs are subtle, and it's up to *you* to pick up on them. Your woman's not going to tell you, "Honey, I'm going to seed," the way she might if she were going to leave. But I've observed how it happens again and again and have interviewed many men who witnessed the decline. The going-to-seed process follows a typical set of stages, each one marked by another disheartening sign. I can tell you what to look for, but *you*'ve got to care enough to *look*.

Many men miss the signals for the very same reasons that the signs appear: because they're not tuned into their woman; they're not minding her state of mind. So one morning men wake up to some less-than-alluring stranger, one who's already died on the vine.

Time is at a premium. The farther the process progresses, the harder it is to reverse. It has an inertia all its own. But if you catch it early enough, you may just be able to turn it around. If you find you can't, you at least know what's ahead and can distribute your eggs into baskets accordingly.

So watch for these changes, and be on the alert.

Stage 1. "She Doesn't Seem Interested in Much Anymore."
Yep, the first sign she's drooping is her energy dropping, at least as far as you're concerned. She doesn't seem to have much to say anymore – nothing special, nothing exciting. Maybe you don't either, but she always was able to grab your interest and get you talking before. You recall when you used to go out together and would never run short of conversation – the deep and meaningful kind. One topic would lead to the next, always leaving loose ends that could lead into others. You'd shake your head sadly at other couples around you – sullen, silent, staring into their salads or commandeering their kids – and *swear you'd never become like that*. But maybe you have, and she *seems* more at fault since she was more open than you to begin with.

She is less active and engaged in her job, her hobbies, and her community work. She's dropped her pilates, her writing, her political action, her dreams of a business. They used to consume her. They made her appealing. They made you take notice, a few times feel threatened, but at other times, you felt challenged to vie for her spotlight. And now, how you wish for that challenge again.

She doesn't seem much interested in sex anymore either. Oh, she's nice about refusing. She's just tired or kind of down. And often enough she says yes. But it's more like you're put off from asking. You wonder where she hid away those slinky negligees and why in the world she'd rather wear those priggish granny nightgowns and Bozo-cut pajamas. And why she won't sit in your lap so often. And why she won't slip into the shower with you. And why she no longer looks longingly at that beautiful body of yours. It hurts to think how long it's been since she said what a dashing figure you sculpt in her favorite three-piece suit. But perhaps what discourages you the most, though you might not have noticed yet, is the fact she seldom *looks* at you – and I mean *really looks* – at your face, into your eyes, and at your crotch and up again. No, nothing puts off like apparent indifference.

Not that you *can't* get her interested. But when you do, it's not quite as wild. Perhaps she's less willing to "do it in the dirt," or in the kitchen, or in the bath, or in the poodle position. The couch is too soft, the carpet's too hard, the idea's too kinky, or the lighting's too bright. She's reluctant to put on a garter and stockings, or drag out her mini-skirt, or wet her white tee-shirt. Then she seems rather shy about showing her pleasure. You're not sure she got off twice, once, or at all. And it's tacky to ask, so you try to dismiss it, and fantasize something to get yourself off.

The *truth* is she hasn't dropped *all* her interests. She's just shifted priorities around. Perhaps she's into baking or babies or house beautiful. They're things you may not notice. They're not part of your world. They don't capture your conversation. I bet you don't perk up at *her* intrigue with the neighbor's Hollandaise sauce recipe, or with Junior's first try at rice, or with the longevity of the philodendron plant. What's most likely is that she's gotten engrossed in the drill march of domesticity, the mechanics of running a home. And if you've had children, for certain she's swamped with relentless requests and mischievous messes. (Here's something that you could relieve.) So you get neglected. And she's always tired and seldom romantic, sexy, or fun.

Remember, too, women don't write the love songs. They aren't the dreamers and poets that you are. They've been socially pulled and situationally pushed to play the *pragmatists* of the species. So they get into efficiency: organizing, managing, tending to daily doldrums, urgencies, and immediacies. Admit it, you know they work hard. If your home is your castle, it's often their *sweat shop*. So sometimes when you see the sign of listlessness, it may mean she's just exhausted. Help shoulder her burdens for a while to see if she doesn't spring back up. That means do the laundry or sweep the floors – show your good faith – then *talk* to her.

If your load-lifting fails to lighten her spirit, you may just be in for a longer-term haul. I talked about women who marry for money; they're easy to please if you bring home the green. There are others who hook up to have a home and raise children. A few even marry to leave lousy jobs or to earn the esteemed M.R.S. degree. So for some women, a man is a *means* to an end – a *marvelous* means, but not their rainbow's end. It's hardly bizarre then if their libido gets lazy in realms of romance, love, and sex. These weren't their highest priorities to begin with; more precious and pressing ones grab center stage.

This trend is so common in marriages with children that it's not a *certain* sign a woman's going to seed. She may or may not be. So don't panic yet. Just keep reading on.

Stage 2. "She's Stopped Flirting With Other Men." *Believe me*, all you men out there, this is *not* something you want to see happen. Ironically enough, this "ultimate reassurance" is a sure sign of ultimate trouble.

Of course, I'm talking about "innocent" flirting, the kind *you* do with other women at work, at parties, in stores, on the street, or if you're so daring, in church or at stoplights. It's the winkish smile, the slipped-in compliment, the eye-locked talk, the careless brushing by – whatever conveys the message, "You remind me that we're members of the opposite sex. You attract me and make me feel a little more alive today." Innocent enough, huh?

Everybody needs this kind of gentle stroke once in a while. When we're feeling confident, we even seek it out. No matter how much love we're getting from our Special Someone, we still need the confirmation of respected Second Opinions. They serve to reassure us that our lover isn't crazy and thus to raise the value of our lover's love for us.

So a woman who stops seeking Second Opinions is no longer boosting the value of *yours*. She may not be feeling attractive enough to put her feminine charms to the test. If she's *that* down on her womanly worth, she may start to feel she's got nothing to lose by letting it slide entirely.

Of course, how alluring your woman feels depends a lot on the opinion that she thinks *you* have of her. She may think it's high, but for all the wrong reasons because, to her, you seem needy, or short on experience, or too easy to please, or simply oblivious to her as a woman. Or maybe she thinks you think well of her only because of the services she renders. Either way, your love doesn't count for much to her – and it doesn't help build her libido and ego – unless it's for what she regards as the "right things" for the "right reasons." We'll look at the right stuff in a little while.

Then again, your woman may value your opinion of her highly and firmly believe that it's *low*. If she's right, you shouldn't be with her. If she's wrong, what *have* you been telling her? Or what have you *not* been telling her?

The most chilling possibility is that she's put her sexuality on ice, so she could care less about men and making their bunson's burn. You know if she's going this route. She yawns at the mention of sex. At the rare times when you get her to do it, all she does is roll over and play dead. If you bring up "the problem" in conversation, she shies away, makes up excuses, or starts a diversionary squabble. Maybe she's stressed out at work. Maybe she's married to motherhood. Or maybe there's something amiss between the two of you, and she's madder than hell at *anything* that can piss standing up. More later on what may be amiss.

Stage 3. "There's More of Her to Love." Beware when a woman abandons her diet. And I don't mean goes off it for special occasions or bounces around in a safe ten-pound range. The woman to watch is the one who jumps dress sizes.

Few men know the difference between a size 5 and size 10, and they wouldn't think of spot-checking her closet if they did. But you *can* tell if she's donning all new duds and doesn't come home excited from shopping sprees. Or if she scowls when you innocently ask her to slip on a certain old sexy little dress that used to harden your arteries. It's also worth finding out where the old wardrobe went. If it's boxed and buried in the basement – well, *maybe* she's thinking of fitting into it again. But if she's gotten *rid* of it and not a thread remains, it means she hasn't the slightest hope or intention of seeing that size again.

As I said before, a woman has to fight off food just to keep her weight at bay. Most of you men are quite sympathetic. You rarely begrudge her an extra ten pounds. And you realize that her winning the weight war doesn't mean she can't concede a few battles. What signifies *surrender* is a *series* of little retreats:

1. After succumbing to holiday splurges, she doesn't go back into battle. She passively accepts the enemy occupation of a few more pounds each season.

2. She starts to justify her increasingly frequent concessions as one-shot "social exigencies." Her excuses are as much to herself as to you: "Ooo, la la! Regardez those Paris pastries. It won't hurt this once, n'est-ce pas?" "We're in too big a hurry for a salad bar. Let's pick up some cheeseburgers, fries, and a shake." "We so rarely dine out in such elegance, it'd be a crime not to splurge, don't you

agree?" "I *had* to take seconds of Aunt Sarah's stroganoff, or her poor widowed heart would have broken." "Guess what we're having for dinner tonight! Remember Katie's incredible recipe for stuffed cannelloni in butter and cream sauce?" "It's such a shame we don't have dessert anymore that...." when the fact is you've skipped it for years for good reason.

    3. When her new eating habits become evident, she gets militant: "It isn't *fair* that women can't eat as much as men do and stay thin." "Women are *supposed* to get heavier with age." "A few extra pounds keep my face from getting lines." "You wouldn't want me to get anorexic, would you?" She's leading her own Tummy Liberation Movement.

    4. Finally, she just stuffs herself freely without explanation. Typically, a woman's surrender on the food front is accompanied by a withdrawal on the exercise front. Whatever helped keep her in shape before – running, hiking, bicycling, walking, swimming, dancing – is progressively abandoned. Sex-ercise suffers as well, but not due to a lack of interest at this stage. Now it's a matter of *pride*. She doesn't want to be seen. In fact, her efforts to hide her body may set off the next stage and make matters worse.

    Stage 4. "She Always Looks Like She's on a Camping Trip." Except she's not tan and vigorous. She seldom wears make-up anymore or your favorite perfume. Jewelry gets in her way, she tells you. And long hair is too hard to keep up, she says. So she lets it get stringy and dingy. Or decides what she needs is a wash-and-wear cut. So she goes to some Buster Brown beauty salon and gets the Marine Sergeant's Special. "Isn't it neat!?" she beams as she runs her hand through the stubble. Being the gentleman that you are, you gallantly grit your teeth and grunt, "I'm glad *you* like it." But all the while you're thinking that she should've gotten the cut on her legs.

    Which reminds you that you've hardly seen her legs for months. She hasn't put on a dress or skirt since Aunt Edna's wedding (or was it her funeral?). In any case, your woman's switched her wardrobe style from soft and slinky to Army Surplus – khaki pants, baggy jeans, worn-out work shirts, stretched-out sweat shirts – whatever can show off her figure the *least*. She's adopted a sluggish posture to match: head down, shoulders slumped, tummy out, one hip cocked so the other can hang. And the spring in her walk has turned into a waddle.

It makes a man long for the good old days when his woman would take half the day to get dressed. Now you feel bad for your gentle complaining. But, believe me, that didn't set off this stage.

She may be trying to conceal those extra pounds she has under her belt from Stage 3. Or perhaps she's attempting to put you off sexually by camouflaging her femininity (an advanced phase of Stage 1 symptoms). She figures you may just *forget* she's a woman. Or she may be forgetting *herself*. She may be so distracted by domestic dictates that she feels she's just dressing for the occasion – the occasion of baby spitting up, of toddler tossing food, of sauce splattering and floor washing. Would *you* wear a suit in the coal mines?

There are, of course, *other* occasions – like candlelit evenings with you, but they're happening less and less. She hasn't been dressing or acting the part, so you haven't been playing yours. No, by now she's lost her Angelina Jolie cool, her Sandra Bullock spunk, and her Julia Roberts dignity, along with all apparent pride in her appearance. In their place are the puffy plainness, a sloppy slouch, and the dim-lit look of a Minnie Mouse.

Stage 5. "*All Her Friends Look Frumpy, Too.*" You can tell a lot about your woman by the female company she keeps. If she intends to stay trim and attractive, she usually hangs out with similarly stunning friends. They help each other make the effort easier. They jog, do aerobics, or work out together and swap nutritional and dieting hints. Then when they feel they've "been good" long enough, they treat themselves to a clothing shopping spree. They may even scheme a women's night out to show off their wares at some watering hole. (Don't worry – they just go there to count the heads they can turn.)

If she's on her way to seed, however, she starts to drop out of her circle of sirens. She comes to see them as "vain," "too slick," or "immature for their age." She drops their activities, too.

You may not even notice the new crowd she's fallen in with; it's not particularly eye-catching. These friends fail to inspire your flirtation or fantasy. And they look all too much like what your woman's becoming.

Well, birds of a feather get frumpy together. They make each other feel that their going to seed is "normal." They reinforce their false hope that only movie stars keep themselves up. They offer each other "living proof" that they can have their man and eat cake, too. (Losing your man or giving up cake may get you kicked out of the flock). When these gals get together, they tend to stay close to the hearth, planning baby showers, swapping home decor ideas, and baking their sin *du jour*. Of course, they go out shopping but *never* for clothes for themselves. (They may not want to know their size or let anyone else know it, either.)

If your woman has gotten to this stage, she's going to be hard to salvage. The social pressure is on her to droop farther faster, and the social support is around to cushion her fall from the vine.

Can Your Garden Be Saved?

Yes! An attentive gardener with a green thumb and a fertile heart has been known to work absolute miracles. You see, unlike a fruit or veggie, a woman's season is never over. She can bloom like an apple blossom all year round, spring after spring. Of course, she won't if she's left to grow wild. And she won't if her home soil is rocky and hard. A woman requires a lot of care and tending, regular exposure to sunny smiles, and frequent floods of compliments.

So if you see your woman going to seed, take heart. Then prepare to take *action*. A woman with Post-Wedding Poop Out *can* be pumped up again. She may need a new goal to get up and go for, and the faith of her man can ignite her. You can stop a woman on the skids of Security Slippage if you raise her respect for herself and your love. You can help lift her out of Living-the-Dream Letdown by setting her sights on new dreams to soar for. You may have the firepower to blow away her Blues if you can get at the bullet she's biting. And you can fill up her Empty Nest Emptiness if you're game to add some new ground to your marriage.

What *won't* work are macho, quick-fix-it home remedies. And they have a history of failure to prove it. For instance, some men have tried "shock therapy" – the zapping news of another woman in the wings or the threat that they're going to leave. While the "patient" is dazed, she may show some improvement, but the shock wears off quickly. And there are ill side effects, including a hangover of hurt and suspicion. Men also have struck out with "physical therapy"; that's beating your woman to make her get better. But she only gets bitter. Besides, it's malpractice.

The effective technologies are slower but surer. They require your patience because inertia is against you. You can *reverse* the process of your woman's going to seed by doing the same things that keep it from *starting*, and you can keep her from going to seed doing the same things that keep her from *going*.

Conversely, you can push her downhill doing the same things that can drive her out the door. Your woman decides her direction, and it's usually one or the other. It depends on how she calculates her resources against her constraints. The seeders rarely wander while the door-watchers keep themselves up for the run. But for a woman, her going to seed is just another form of going, a less dramatic way of dealing with an insufferable situation. As far as *you're* concerned, it's just another way of *losing* her, one that simply spreads out the payments over time.

The stages along the separate ways of seeding and leaving are different. The signs to look out for are different, too – often quite the opposite. So we'll look at the symptoms of her leaving next. Then we'll get down to the business of what men do to lose their woman, one way or the other, and what you can do to keep your own lovely lively and living with you.

Chapter 6.

How to Tell She's Going – Before You Lose Her

Most men don't read the signs very well. Or they get the picture too late. So they don't know what hit them when the door slams behind her. "Why did she leave?" they ask in utter bewilderment. "Hell, nothing *seemed* wrong between us. I came home every night, and we had dinner. We hadn't had a fight in weeks. *I* was happy. I didn't know *she wasn't*."

Don't be defensive. It's a simple fact that women initiate more break-ups than men, that men typically weren't aware that their woman was unhappy, and that they can't figure out why she left. As a result, they mourn their loss a lot longer and harder than she mourns hers. It's not that men are *ignorant*, but they are frightfully *innocent* in the ways of women and love.

Of course, there are many reasons why men are so often caught by surprise:

1. She's sly. Most women withdraw and even get cagey when they're thinking of leaving. They're *angry* at their man for not noticing or responding to their expressions of dissatisfaction. At the same time, they would still like the relationship to work. They give their man every chance they can tolerate. So they may act like nothing's up so they can keep open their options to leave or not to leave.

2. He's threatened. For a lot of understandable reasons, men don't want to see that a problem exists. Some fear making the changes they sense their woman wants; hell, it's work! And it holds the possibility of failure. Others simply aren't *willing* to make the changes they think are necessary – at least not until she suddenly disappears. Still others don't *know* what to do or how to change, and feel powerless.

In any case, *all* men feel their egos and life style so threatened by the prospect of losing their woman that they silently panic and run blind in the opposite direction. They'll try to rationalize the problem away and chalk it up to *her* irrationality: "overreaction," "too emotional," "110% female," "job's got her down," "kids driving her crazy," "on the rag," "early change of life." Remember sitting with the guys at the bar bemoaning how crazy women get? If they're *really* so nuts, why do you love them so much? Men will even do the most love-destructive things to release their frustrations: make jealous accusations, cut back the household budget, curtail sex and other expressions of love, even get physically violent. Unfortunately, these are the very things that drive her out the door even faster.

3. She's better than ever. Be warned and beware! Some of the signs that she's ready to leave make her *more attractive* to her man. She's not complaining, she looks great, and she seems happy. Only she's *not* being more attractive *for her man* – not the one she's leaving. He takes this terminal sign for just the opposite, and he winds up really faked out.

So let's lay out some of the signs to look for. There are stages to the process of losing your woman. So pay special attention to the early ones. Someday you might be awfully glad you did.

The Early Warning Signs

Almost *all* women *tell* you very *plainly* first that there's a cancer growing on your intimacy. But the *explicit* message may confuse you. She tells you that *she's* losing *you* – *your* attentiveness, *your* commitment, *your* love, and the "you" she fell in love with. But you don't feel lost at all. So you respond with a baffled "huh?" followed by a curt reassurance that *of course* you still love her – and go back to your newspaper. You *heard* her right, but you didn't *read* her right. *You're* beginning to lose *her*. But you've got a little time. Watch for these stages.

Stage 1: "The Hopeful Wooing-You-Back Phase." She suggests starting "new communication patterns" and tries to initiate heart-to-heart talks. She insists on just-the-two-of-us dinners, perhaps by candlelight or in restaurants you can barely afford. She starts pushing for romantic mini-trips and cruises to exotic places you can't find on a map. She shows a sudden rise in sexual interest. She gets a new black negligee, initiates some kinky new variation, and suggests you do it in the oddest place.

She wants a *response* out of you – energy, attention, romance, *action*. But if these signs are ignored:

Stage 2: "The Tearful Laying-It-Out-Phase." She cries, whines, and mopes around a lot. She spends evenings either sadly cuddled up to you like an abandoned puppy or weepily bitching and nagging about what's wrong with the two of you, why don't you do this or that anymore, etc. Her sexual interest is inexplicably on-again, off-again, from irrepressible to unarousable.

Now she *desperately* needs a response out of you, and her sense of powerlessness is showing. She's losing her self-possession and can't help it. On the other hand, *you're* losing your *woman*, and still *can* help it. But if these signs are ignored:

Stage 3: "The Angry Let-Him-Have-It-Phase." She doesn't look at you – *really look* at you – much anymore. She's frenetically occupied with household tasks – everything but fixing your favorite dinners. She slights you in subtle ways (your socks aren't matched), makes snide little digs at your competency (you think you cut the grass the same way you always do), and laughs loudest at the bitterest jokes about love and men. Yet she's as nice as ever to everyone else – maybe even nicer. Sex? She's got every tried-and-untrue excuse in the book: "a headache," "too tired," "my period," dead silence.

Since at least the house is a little quieter than it was during Stage 2, some men think the problem is blowing over. Actually, it's gotten worse, *far worse*. And, it's just about to get *worse still* if you just sit there. She's *mad* now, just about ready to give up. And you know that hell hath no fury like a woman ignored. So if you blow off these early signs, get ready for...

The Advanced Warning Signs

Time is running out. You may or may not be too late. That depends on how fast other options materialize for her and what you're willing to do. These signs *tend* to show up in order, but they don't *have* to. So don't think you've still got slack because she's only on #3. And not all these signs need appear before she *dis*appears.

"She Shuts Up." Ah, peace at last, you think. The *most dangerous, surest sign* is when she finally *stops bothering* to tell you what's wrong. She also probably stops harping about all the harm your eating and drinking are doing to yourself. In fact, she heaps on the fried potatoes and gravy for you! Hell, why should she care? *She's given up on you.* She barely gives a rat's ass whether you live or die. In *her* eyes, you've ignored her, misunderstood her, confined her, or failed to take her seriously for far too long. But she's still got her pride, and she isn't giving away any more of her power to *you*.

Unfortunately, most men read the silence for just the opposite. It may be pleasant for a while, but the next thing you'll hear is the door slamming behind her.

"She's Forgetful about You." These slights aren't *purposeful* like in the Early Warning Stage 2. By now, she's proudly succeeded to *forget* your favorite beer, your Sunday dinner, your laundry, and all those countless little things you've depended upon her for. Don't they seem *big* now? It's getting very late, isn't it?

"She's Gone a Lot." She's chronically late from work. She goes shopping more, especially when *you're home*. Or she gets passionately entranced with some haywire hobby like pot-throwing or some contrived cause like Save the Snails. In any case, she's always gone for hours at a time. Well, maybe she's a true devotee of something, and maybe she's not. Maybe she's off doing something else. No, she's not necessarily having an affair. If she is, she'll also give off the signs below. But the point is, she's sure avoiding being with *you*.

"She's on a Self-Improvement Kick." Unless she's on one with you – especially if you're looking a little paunchy and frayed around the edges – count your *days*, not your blessings. You may love her even more for having shed those pounds, toned those muscles, fixed up her hair, gotten that tan, and broadened her interests. But enjoy it while it lasts. She's getting ready to fly – away. And if she's not already bound for another man's arms, she's scouting the territory for a new nest.

"She's Awfully Happy About Something." If you can't figure out what it is, and she isn't saying, you can bet it's *not you*. If this sign shows up along with most of the others, you've probably been replaced.

What's particularly confusing about her final warning signal is that, out of the blue, she may start treating you *better*. Or so it may seem. Amid weeks of utterly ignoring you, she may suddenly seduce you on the dining room table, or serve you a romantic feast in her negligee, or surprise you with some sweet but off-the-wall gift. But don't be too reassured. She might be feeling a little guilty about her first visit to her lawyer. Or she might want you to remember her fondly – *so* fondly that you'll want to jump off the Tallahatchie Bridge when she goes. Or perhaps she's missing her lover; if you can't be with the one you love, love the one you're stuck with, right? Or maybe she's so overflowing with love for her new romance that she has some left over *even* for *you*.

I know it hurts. But don't forget that it hurt *her* too, just as deeply – only way back during those Early Warning Stages that *you* sat out.

When Is It Terminal?

So she left. It's *really* quiet now. Deadly so. Except for the gentle cracking of ice cubes in your warm whiskey. Put the bottle down. Now's the perfect time to think.

First, you've got to figure out *why* she left. The next chapter will tell you how men tend to *miscast* the reasons. The one after that will help set you straight with an array of leads. Then Chapter 9 lays out what you should have been doing all along. Prescriptions for dealing with particular circumstances, like children and the liberated woman, follow in Chapters 10 and 11.

Now you have two choices. You can either try to get her back, or you can let go. If you're game for the former, check out Chapter 12. It doesn't carry any *guarantee* you'll get her back, but at least you won't blow it. First, you're going to really research the specifics of why she left you. You'll have to ask her and her friends for "the awful truth." And no one will tell you the real truth if there's any hint you'll react defensively, vengefully, violently, or anything but *totally open*. To find out the score, you'll have to approach her, *just once*, exactly the way she was nagging you to before.

In any case, you should look at Chapter 13, "When to Let Go," to decide how terminal the situation is. Some differences just can't be resolved, and there's no use even trying. That's okay. There're plenty of other fine women to love out there. In fact, it's a man's market. According to the U.S. Census Bureau, 54% of all unmarried and single Americans were women in 2004. And as you go up the age ladder, the stats just keep getting better for you. Take heart. And this next time, you'll be much wiser in the ways of women.

Chapter 7.

What a Man Thinks *Has Happened When He Loses His Woman*

Too many men can face contemplating their loss only through the smoky brown haze of whiskey in a bar. (At least Jack Daniels can understand.) Even when they do dare to look at their problem in the crystal-clear light of sobriety, they're blinded by the reflection of the loss of their woman on *themselves*. A man feels he's lost not only his mistress, maid, second mommy, moral mentor, and whatever else she meant to him, but also the respect of his friends, his own self-respect, and in the most stark and naked terms, his very balls. Losing his woman carries heavy *social* as well as personal costs.

As I pointed out at the beginning of this book, most men tragically never really understand why they lose their woman. They can't fathom what's been going on in her head, or they err in reading her cues. What they wind up doing is muttering a hopeless, "I don't know" or spinning some pretty superficial theories. Not that they can't learn; they just never get a chance to, or they're scared they'll have to change drastically. Actually, few men have to change much; it's usually "the little things" that mean the most to a woman, or that drive her away.

But amid the ignorance and fears, men typically foster some pretty wrong ideas, often among themselves, as to why they lose their woman. They tend to dump on themselves too heavily or blame their woman too exclusively. Let's look at some of these man-made myths, recognizing the grain of truth some may contain.

The "I'm to Blame" Reasons: Guilt

This is usually a man's first stage of dealing with the loss. But what he blames himself for being or doing may or may not reflect what has actually been bugging his woman.

"I wasn't a good enough provider." That depends upon how *steady* a provider you've been, and what you led her to *expect* you'd

provide. You men tend to measure your personal worth *too* much in monetary terms, whether in the boardroom or the bedroom. But it's also true that a woman looks mostly to her man to make their collective "mark on the world." Even if she works, her social status still depends on you, too. But she's only likely to feel frustrated and powerless if you promised her a lot more than you've delivered. Even so, if that's *the* reason she left you, and *all* you were to her was a meal ticket and prestige peacock, consider yourself lucky to have lost her.

"I wasn't attractive enough." But you attracted her at the start. You may have a point if you've let yourself go physically, especially if she hasn't. But even so, you can bet that's not the whole story. A partner's looks mean less to a woman than to a man. So beware of projecting your own headset onto hers.

"I couldn't fulfill her sexually." Now we're getting somewhere. But men tend to define the *specific* problem in terms of their *own* securities: "I couldn't get it up often enough." "I couldn't keep it up long enough." "My penis is too small." In all my intimate talks and interviews with women, *not once* did penis size concern them. Women care *much* more about *quality* than quantity. But more about that later.

"I gave too much." What you *really* mean here is that you fear you bargained away your power by being "too nice," "too attentive," "too loving" – that is, you got pussy-whipped. Well, you *can't* be too nice to a woman, any more than you can be too rich. I've never even *heard* of a woman who mocked her man for being at her beck and call. (Women *brag* about their men when they are.) Pussy-whip paranoia is strictly a mental illness cultivated by the male subculture.

It's true that there are a few fawning puppy dogs, but they lose a woman because they treat them like their domineering mother. Don't worry about falling into this select group of men unless you act guilty when you can't clean your plate or you can't flush the toilet without your woman's approval.

"I wasn't macho enough." This is the Real Man's version of "I gave too much," since Real Men don't give *anything*. Anyway, the way men tend to define macho – the devil-may-care, bar-brawling stud who thinks passion means taciturn toughness – has no appeal to any self-respecting woman (that is, the kind worth keeping). If women *did* like macho, they'd act that way themselves. So much for the macho myth.

The "She's to Blame" Reasons: Bitterness

After a man beat himself up, more often than not for the wrong reasons, he usually turns around and pins the whole mess on his woman, at least for a time. While just as incomplete a picture as the first-stage blame game, this second stage of dealing with the loss is less painful. The man feels self-justified and even a bit glad to be rid of her – and sometimes he should be.

"She changed all of a sudden." Maybe she *did* change, but it probably wasn't all of a sudden. You probably missed the signs described in Chapter 6. Come to think of it, *you* might have changed, too – if not in your heart, then in your behavior. Remember way back in Chapter 1, I talked about how most men become less romantic and less attentive to their woman after slipping into the security of having won her? Of course, you didn't *mean* to; you didn't even *notice* it. But *she* did. Maybe you only noticed her change in response to yours.

"She didn't know what she wanted." If she was especially young and impressionable when you got together, you might very well be on the right track. Deciding what we *really want* in a mate, a job, or anything else involves resolving all those traditional values our parents and teachers *indoctrinated* in us, with all those exotic, new-fangled goals our youth culture *dared* us to go for. Getting the over-lap into focus for ourselves takes time. So maybe you're too much what her *mother* wanted, in which you might look *her* up after the pain subsides, or maybe not enough.

In any case, if this is part of the problem, have a little sympathy for your woman. From the tenderest ages on, women are under considerable pressure to catch a man; that and motherhood proves her womanhood. Sometimes the pressure even breaks her spirit, and she settles for what's expedient and available rather than what's best for her.

But just as you seriously pondered your eventual line of work, women are just as serious about deciding on their type of man – and often their line of work as well. Most women, the mature ones anyway, know *exactly* what they want in a man. They can rattle off his traits, tastes, interests, and life goals faster and more specifically than you can recite your own. Of course, they can compromise, and they almost always do, each according to her own elaborate calculus that only a computer could replicate as quickly.

The point is that, unless she was young, it's doubtful your woman *didn't* know what she wanted when she decided on you. But whatever that was and is today, you're not it now.

"She's Impossible to Please. She Demanded Too Much." That must make you Mr. Perfect, doesn't it? But to be fair, it *is* true that women demand a lot more out of a love relationship than you do, and they're usually less happy with the one they're in than are you. So if your woman always seemed less overjoyed than you by the simple things in life – like a six pack of Heineken's and Monday Night Football – you weren't imaging things.

But let's face it, men, most of you ask for *very little* – a well-run household with cold beer, children who know when to get out of your way, and your woman within calling distance. In turn, you give about what you ask for. That's not unfair. But she's not being unfair asking for more either because she's probably willing to give it, maybe even *desperate* to give it. All too much, women are taught in get-your-man "training" magazines, from *Seventeen* to *Cosmopolitan*, to give, give, give to their man. Dress for him. Cook for him. Learn how to tighten your vagina for him. And so plenty of them try. But there are no such manuals *for you* men telling *you* what to give to *her*. There's no glossy magazine next to *Road and Track* called *Debonair* or *Savvy Hunk*, is there?

There's only one tiny class of women who *may* be impossible to please, and that's the True Neurotic. She's *never* pleased by *anything* – not her kid's straight "A" report card ("Why didn't you get an A – in P.E.?"), not your last promotion ("You should have gotten this years ago."), not even a sale at Bloomingdale's ("Everything was picked over, only 50% off, and I couldn't find a place to park.") If you have one of these rare breeds and you *want* to keep her, I advise how to do best with this bad situation in Chapter 11, "Special Cases." But if you just lost one, count your blessings.

The "We're to Blame" Reasons: Detached Rationality

It's a sign of his heart healing well when a man advances to this final stage of explaining the loss. Most of you men come around to seeing that it takes *two* to make or break a relationship. Even if *she* left *you*, you can look back and recall that maybe *you* weren't all that happy with *her* either. You start blaming the problem on the "negative dynamics" that developed between the two of you: "We stopped communicating." "We didn't share enough interests." "We wanted different things out of life." "We weren't compatible." "We drifted apart." While exceptions exist, a mutual parting of the minds account for break-ups better than anything else.

At about this stage of thinking, you want to get out from under the hurt, hatred, and recriminations and start putting your life back together again. That's all fine and good, but a lot of you are in a mighty big hurry to wrap up this matter – loose ends still hanging out – and forget it. You'll try to find that straight-line shortest distance between pain and feeling good again: rationality.

Men are very attached to the notion of rationality. They believe it prevents or solves every problem short of baldness. And logically speaking, if you're not totally to blame, and she's not either, then it must be *both* of you together. Swell. But that's as far as logic alone will take you. All those "we screwed up" conclusions may be accurate, but they're just surface-level clichés and certainly not the last word on the matter. They're just *beginnings*, because *they don't tell you how to keep yourself from winding up in the same whiskey haze over some other woman again.*

They don't tell you *how* or *why* you and your woman stopped communicating, lost common ground, and drifted apart. They don't give you and the true dynamic of what each of you did and didn't do to one another to wind up on unbridgeable shores. They make you-as-a-couple sound like some mystical third entity which had a problem – not you or her – and lets both of you off the hook for taking responsibility for your actions.

Nor do the we-rationales tell you what *you* can do differently *next* time to keep communication flowing, interests growing, and passion burning. Not that a woman doesn't have her part to play, too. But if *you* know what *you're* doing on *your* side, you can inspire her to catch and carry the ball with fewer fumbles on *her* side.

So in the next chapter, we're going to look at the kinds of things that men do, or fail to do, that make their woman drop the ball, and later leave the game.

Chapter 8.

What's Really *Happening:*
How a Man Loses His Woman

What's *really* happening has to be seen through the *woman's* eyes, if she's the one who decides to do the leaving. It's not that her eyes are necessarily any clearer than yours. But you have to know what *she* sees that *she* needs and how *she* sees *you* to understand how you can lose her.

We can boil down the male behaviors that drive almost all women away to five basic "faults," as women see them. Let's call them the 5-I's:

        1. Irresponsibility
        2. Indifference
        3. Intimidation
        4. Inconsistency
        5. Insensitivity

These 5-I's are pretty vague and abstract in themselves. But in various combinations and permutations, they shape twelve different "syndromes" of male behavior that might sound more familiar. If you see yourself in any of them, you're likely to be in a lot of trouble with your woman sooner or later.

"Tragic Flaws"

Let's not portray you as a "tragic hero" á la Hamlet. We're talking here about hard core, get-your-act-together personal problems that you can and should do something about. *Not* to fix yourself is completely irresponsible. And in your more lucid moments, you know it. The "flaws" at issue here are active alcoholism, drug abuse, chronic gambling, compulsive eating, treatable mental illness, and the inability to hold a job. Of course, some of these are interrelated. Alcoholism or drug abuse may lurk behind your intermittent unemployment. Mental illness may cause your passive-aggressiveness with authority figures or your irrepressible urges to bet the farm on the horses. With the exception of a few mental illnesses (schizophrenia, for example), these problems do have cures and solutions if you're willing to work and maybe pay for them. Either you run them or they'll run you. Choosing the latter is a sure-fire way to lose a woman, and she'll get all the sympathy.

"Losing by Intimidation"

Trying to "beat her into line" or "slap some sense into her," are you? Yeah, sure, like that'll work. I'm talking here about psychological as well as physical intimidation, about bully tactics like four-letter name-calling, telling her she's just like her mother (just to set her off balance and give yourself a chance to win), and other ways of not fighting fair. If you're honest with yourself, you'll admit you do it out of runaway frustration and disgust with *yourself*, not your woman. You may be jealous of her or feel upstaged by her. Deep down, you know you're in the wrong striking out at her. But you do it anyway. You've got a problem.

As you may already know, the law has a name for *any* form of touching, directly or with an object, that she does not consent to: battery. Only self-defense or defense of another person will get off. In fact, there's a name for just *threatening* to harm another person: assault. Women are a lot less hesitant to call the police and to prosecute either crime than they used to be. So if you're a wife-batterer, even "a little bit," you're putting *yourself* as well as your woman in jeopardy. Besides, wife-battering usually starts as "a little bit" and accelerates over time to causing genuine personal injury, even death, whether intended or not, as well as acting violent in public. Since the vast majority of wife-battering goes on behind closed doors, its prevalence is uncertain. But it does cross racial, ethnic, and socioeconomic class lines.

Amazingly enough, most women will tolerate being battered for months, even years. Some believe the behavior is aberrant and will go away; it won't. Some think they can figure out how to stop it by saying or doing just the right thing in response; they can't. A few women may even come to the conclusion that they must deserve it, even if they can't fathom what they have done to provoke it. (Actually the only way a woman can possibly "deserve" it is to be so violent to her man or someone else that he acts in self-defense or defense of another.) Whatever excuse for staying in the relationship a woman has, she has stumbled into the "battered woman syndrome." It can happen to even the most accomplished and capable women. The condition is temporary, however. The woman will either come to her senses and leave the batterer or die at his hand. Her life depends on getting away, and everyone who knows her or her man will support her, not him.

No one can help the wife-batterer but himself. He has to own up to his problem and see a therapist. Typical therapy often doesn't work – wife-battering is as stubborn a problem as alcoholism – but there are specialists and support groups that can help.

"Going AWOL"

Call this crime "felony indifference" or "insensitivity in the first degree." Here you're neglecting your woman on a regular basis by making yourself emotionally unavailable to her. Maybe you're not spending enough time at home, meaning not as much as you used to and she grew accustomed to expecting. Or maybe you're physically at home enough, but you isolate yourself and won't interact with her. You act disinterested in her daily life and concerns – not looking at her while she talks to you, not asking her questions about her day, and not responding to her questions. Or you withdraw and stop communicating with her about your own life – in effect, rejecting her as a confidant. If you're not sharing your own life, you probably aren't sharing your good feelings toward her either. Loving her without verbalizing it isn't very convincing to her. .

It doesn't matter that much *how* or *why* you're gone – whether you're a workalcoholic, addicted to sports, possessed by a hobby, hooked on outings with "the boys," or involved with another woman. Same result: She'll start building her own life around anybody and anything but you.

"Coitus Intermittus"

Sadly, you can lose your woman by not making love with her enough. What a nasty turnaround from those teen years, huh. A man's drooping desire can stem from a variety of other problems:

infidelity, alcohol or drugs (see above), or ego problems (that is, the need for conquest). What television ads euphemistically nickname "ED" for erectile dysfunction is often (though not always) treatable with drugs, *if* you can tolerate the side effects.

Of course, "enough" making love depends on her preferences, libido, and expectations, and only you can gauge those. Whatever frequency falls short in her eyes, it makes a woman feel rejected as a lover, even when unintended, and stuck into a sister or roommate role. Many women need more sex more than you do, especially in their 30s and 40s. But it's scary for a woman to initiate sex because a man can rarely get it up if he's not in the mood or feels pressured.

This issue isn't just about male infidelity. A few women expect a man to cheat on them at one time or another. It doesn't shock them to read the statistics that about half of you married fellows stray at least once. And most of you do it pretty "innocently," from a woman's point of view – with a prostitute, a one-night-stand, or some casually encountered cutie at work or your local hangout. Your ego gets fed, but you rarely go for broke and fall in love the way women tend to. So many women, being the bigger gamblers in love, tend to be surprisingly tolerant of your nickel-and-dime ventures. (Of course, if you realize you're gay, you have to come out to her and stop using her as your front.)

What women *d*o demand, though, is that you have enough saved up for *her*. This means that, if you have an affair, you share your sexual good fortunes with her. Unless age has slowed your down, spreading the wealth isn't so difficult since good sex begets more sex. In fact, there's nothing like a fresh affair to make your dick feel like 16 again. If, however, you often prefer to rendezvous with your right hand, you're engaging in one of the most insidious forms of cheating to a woman. Women regard your sexual output as a precious resource which shouldn't be wasted as run-off. Not that there's anything to the myth that you have just so many ejaculations stored in your holster. They're much more like pinballs: The more you play, the more you keep on winning pinballs to keep playing with. The more orgasms you have, the more orgasms you *can* have (within Olympic limits, of course). The point is, put your "precious resource" where it wins the most appreciation and keeps you out of domestic bankruptcy.

"Daddy Dearest"

Don't assume her heart belongs to Daddy if you've been paternalistic or patronizing towards her. This means you haven't been taking her concerns and complaints seriously, especially those about you. It means dismissing her opinions out of hand and discrediting them with *ad womanim* arguments that point to stereotypical female flaws like flakiness, irrationality, and emotionality. Guys, get real. A self-respecting woman simply won't put up with that. What you're actually doing is rejecting her as a friend and an equal adult. It's so 1950s.

"No Room of Her Own"

Ever have a woman break up with you because she needed her "space"? That gal may or may not have been telling you the truth, but your woman definitely needs space. In fact, she has the same needs as *you* do for a piece of her life that's her very own. After all, you have *your* own buddies, *your* own flirtations, *your* own job, and *your* own time alone watching the tube, tinkering in the garage, and even commuting to and from work. (One transportation survey in the Los Angeles megalopolis found people's desire to have time alone in their car their biggest objection to car pooling.) Chances are when you're off on *your* own, she is tending to the kids, which you well know is hardly time alone. Or she is cleaning the house, which is hardly quality time. Ditto for her "stolen moments" shopping and running errands. No, she needs *quality time* alone and on her own, without you sniffing around to find out what she's up to. Go ahead, ask her if she needs more time alone during your quality time together, and don't scold or snicker at her response.

Unfortunately, this private time business is one that many couples are out of sync on. When you men want it the *most*, typically early in a relationship, women want it the *least*. They want more time with *you*. But as you both grow older together, you want it *less* while she wants it *more*. It's not that she's sick of you. She's just realizing what you felt more strongly at the start – that you can't build your life too exclusively around your love. So you poured a lot of energy into your work, "the guys," your hobbies, and such. (In fact, you tend to spread yourself pretty thin in your 20s and 30s). Then you go to make your mark in your world. But you start to see that all these other activities don't make much sense unless they're complemented by time with your woman. Meanwhile, she's been raising kids and expanding her horizons to make the best use of the time she has when you're off on your own. Finally, years later, you come home. She's glad to see more of you and can probably think of 101 things for you to fix up, paint, get rid of, and clean out that might have needed doing ten years ago. Then she goes off on *her* own. Well, let's be fair. You had *your* time when you wanted it; you *took* it. Now she needs and deserves hers. And if you don't give it, she'll take it.

So you may be losing your woman if you're denying her any of her basic freedoms. These include the freedom to hang out with her own friends and even to mix socially with male friends and colleagues. If you raise objections, you're being insufferably possessive. Another inalienable right she has is the autonomy to pursue her own interests, whether hobbies, education, or a career. She also needs time alone doing whatever – none of your business. You might have to pick up a little of the household slack while she's "off." But better to pick up a little now than the whole shebang after she gets to feeling suffocated and leaves. As the wise Eastern sage, Kahil Gibran, advised about marriage in *The Prophet*, "let there be spaces in your togetherness" – or else.

"Promise Her Anything, But..."

Have you proven yourself to be an unrealistic Dreamer? Have you blown up your abilities, your ambitions, and your chances of future success? Have you subsequently raised, then frustrated, her expectations for your life style together? Have you promised her more attention, more household help, more money, gifts, a vacation, or changes in your behavior, and then failed to come through? Have you kept telling her, year after year, that living the Dream is just around the corner? If so, start kissing your woman goodbye.

Most of you men have genuinely good intentions when you dream about your future and promise your woman to deliver what she wants. However, some men use these techniques in a desperate attempt to smooth things over with their women. In the former case, you're fooling yourself, and in the latter, trying to fool *her*, for want of a better approach. But as most of you have already learned, perhaps painfully, it's very difficult to fool a woman. Oh, it may be easy *early* in a relationship, but *not later on*, not after she knows you sometimes better than you know yourself. Then you wind up with a double-barreled debacle; she's mad at you for having disappointed her *and* for having tried to fool either her or yourself.

For all their mystery and magic, women are as mundanely practical as Earth Mothers. Yours will stop dreaming with you if you're not actively *working* towards and *moving* towards the goals you claim. Besides, Dreamers leave themselves open for the most traumatic mid-life crisis.

"Promise Her Nothing" or "The Passive Male Syndrome"

This sure-fire way to alienate your woman sometimes follows the "Promise Her Anything" routine as a disaster recovery strategy. Some men decide that since promising their women good things got them into trouble, they won't promising anything – not even commitment. But more typically, the Passive Male Syndrome develops on its own out of a man's fear of intimacy, chronic indecisiveness, or a felt inability to follow through on commitments. Its distinguishing features are holding back expressions of love and reassurance, your dreams for the future, and commitments of any kind, especially at key commitment-making junctures in the relationship. If this describes you, this syndrome has probably left a series of your relationships in ruins.

To a woman, the Passive Male isn't fair. He's a now-he's-in-it-now-he's-not fair-weather lover, and he sticks all of the "work" of the relationship on her. She takes all the emotional risks building the commitment and expressing love for both of you. Then when something goes wrong, she gets all the blame. The job demands too much ego investment and returns too little for almost any woman in the long run. Emotional withholding also upsets a relationship's "natural rhythm" of progressive commitment-building. Without a build-up, it runs out of steam and collapses – that is, the woman leaves.

"You're So Vain"

Among the many things that a woman can be to a man is a status symbol, like the trophy wife. She has to be stunningly beautyful (usually blond), younger than he is (sometimes scandalously so), seemingly devoted and faithful to him (no visible indiscretions), and completely dependent on him for whatever she values. Such a prize bestows on a man prestigious Alpha-dog status among other men and an ego-flattering symbol of his savvy, his sex appeal, or, most commonly, his bulging bank account. Of course, he may very well replace her with a younger model in ten to twenty years. But that's only if she stays that long.

A man may lose his women precisely because he treats her primarily like an ornamental social object, as a flashy complement to his new Porsche and Armani suit. Only he's very careful to keep his Porsche shiny and well-tuned and to accessorize his suit with Gucci ties and Borges shirts. By contrast, his woman *du jour* gets just enough attention to entice her into committing to him. After all, the vain man usually doesn't plan to keep any *one* woman *too* long, maybe not even as long as he'll keep his Porsche (which he probably leases). He'd rather keep several women on the line and reel them in for his ego amusement every once in a while. In a word, he's a habitual, self-justified, died-in-the-wool cheat (reminiscent of a certain sports figure who turned out to be cheating on the women he was cheating with). The vain man is in fact playing the aggressive peacock's version of Promise Her Nothing.

He may look like the man who has everything, but he's missing something very important: his touch with reality. He's obviously petrified of commitment and intimacy, but he doesn't feel that way. And his love is obviously selfish, ego-centered, and superficial, but he can't see it. This "new narcissism" gets old with a woman pretty quickly.

"Blowing with the Wind"

Here is the man who takes the path of least resistance. He displays no character, integrity, or moral backbone. Either he won't stand up for any principles or values, or he blithely goes against principles or values he has declared. He's a weasel at work, a snake in business dealings, and untrustworthy with friends. With his woman, he's Peter Pan – childish, irresponsible, and ultimately weak inside. He's capable of doing just about anything, as long as it entails the least amount of psychic effort.

He's definitely not what a woman wants. She wants a man with character, or she loses respect. Consider all the male hero sex symbols that captivate the heart-throbbing admiration of millions of women. They do it not by the bulge of their biceps or their bedroom eyes but by the uncompromising character and irreproachable integrity they display in the most dangerous situations. Think the Lone Ranger, Braveheart, Spiderman, "Peace, Justice, and the American Way." Not up to those standards? If you crawl so low than you come off like one of the "bad guys" – well, you know what women think of them. Go ahead – make her day.

"Familiarity Breeds Contempt"

This kind of familiarity grows like mold from the things that Real Men *really* do – things like being crude, crass, and gross in speech and personal habits, acting like a slob (expecting a woman to constantly pick up after you), and letting yourself go physically. In essence, it's acting like an Animal House fraternity boy.

Women are not squeamish little old ladies, and you don't have to always ask them to "pardon your French." They speak French these days, too. But they do have their limits. They lack your locker-room socialization. They are thoroughly unimpressed by noisy displays of flatulence. They reach their limit with dirty jokes, scatological humor (about the ass), and four-letter words before you do.

On the whole, women are not fanatical sanitation engineers either. A few are actually slobs themselves, or they become that way after they stop devoting their lives to picking up after everyone else in the household. But in *most* homes, women are neater and cleaner than men. They see the accumulation of mildew in the shower months before you notice a creature encroachment. They're aware of the greasy fingerprints bordering the woodwork, cabinets, and refrigerator long before you realize those things are *supposed* to be white. They're bothered by the filth and mess, but they're even more bothered that you don't see them and don't do anything about them. You can blame your mothers, if you want. Unfortunately, they tended to pick up after you with little more than a grumble.

On the positive side, women have become more and more attuned to the finer aspects of men's bodies, as well as the not-so-fine aspects. Or they have just grown more open about admitting what they've been looking at all along. Certainly you've noticed the proliferation of male buns magazines and pin-up calendars. There aren't that many Amazon women into Johnny-Weismuller-size muscles. But their eyes avert from the plush paunch (otherwise known as the beer belly) and the distended derriere (commonly called the fat ass).

So these are the not-uncommon-enough syndromes that send a woman packing. In some cases, it takes more than one of these to do it, and I listed the most compelling ones first. But men who lose their women, especially *good* women, have often accumulated several in varying degrees by the time Judgment Day comes.

Now you know what *not* to do to keep your woman. But not being a jerk isn't quite enough, especially to keep your woman the way you love her. So let's turn to the positive things you can do and be to keep her, or even make her back into, the woman of your dreams.

Chapter 9.

How a Man Can Keep Her –
And Keep Her the Way He Loves Her

The topic of "what a woman wants" seems to hold so much mystery for you men that it spawned a very popular Hollywood movie. So let's get right to the point. Here are *ten sure-win things* you can do to keep your woman, along with hints on how to do them. They get to the heart of what a woman really wants from her man. And there's nothing mysterious about them.

1. Trust Her and Be Trustworthy.

Like a man, a woman wants to be trusted. By trusting her, I mean sincerely believing that she cares about you and has your mutual interests at heart—in other words, taking the love she says she has for you at face value.

One aspect of trust is not getting paranoid or suspicious when she's late from work, preoccupied with her laptop, or too tired to cook or do the laundry. These days women work the same hours that men do *and also* do most of the housework and child-caring. Time may be more precious to her than money. Her complicated world cannot revolve around tending to your desires or your schedule. Nor does it focus on you alone. When she's giggling on the phone with one of her girlfriends, don't flatter yourself to think she's making fun of you. Remember that she has her own life to lead, so let her, and don't feel threatened.

Trusting her also means not getting jealous and possessive when she smiles at another man or pauses to appreciate his tightly-packaged ass. Don't you consider it your right to gaze at an alluring female? You're just having a piece of eye-candy, right? Well, she enjoy sweets every once in a while, too. No use reading any more into it.

In turn, you should be as trustworthy yourself as you want her to be. Lead *your* own life with your and her mutual interests at heart. Keep her confidences. Ask for her advice. Don't give her reasons to doubt your commitment due to any of the five I's: Irresponsibility, Indifference, Intimidation, Inconsistency, and Insensitivity. Remember, they're at the heart of what really sends a woman packing (or kicking you out).

If your woman hasn't been showing you love in a convincing way, let her know it and tell her how you would like her to show it. Either she'll tell you it's too late, the relationship is dead on the vine and you should have read Chapter 6 earlier, or she'll thank you and give your suggestions a try. If she loves you, she wants to reassure you. And remember, women *like* to talk about this kind of stuff. It doesn't make them squirm at all.

2. Show Respect for Her World and Share in It.

Many men treat the woman's world as if it's a cute, frivolous joke. It's gift-wrapping, button-sewing, silver-polishing, nose-powdering, window-shopping frou-frou. Well, it may be some or even all of those things, but it's a lot more, too. The woman's world is broader and more sophisticated than ever before, and women think better of it than ever before. It includes career, budgeting, home repair, politics, the economy, and international affairs as well as home decorating, child-rearing, and shopping. Women expect you to respect it and participate in it with them.

Granted, women know how miserable and forlorn you look when they take you shopping for things other than hardware and cars. Well, get over it. At least, act a little interested. Your woman brought you along with her for a reason – probably a better reason than just carrying her bags. Typically, she wants your opinion on products, whether these be appliances, clothes, toys, books, artwork, drapes, or carpeting. You should take this as a compliment. She thinks you have decent, if not excellent, taste and wants you to be happy with the ultimate selection. And don't tell me you don't care. You care *plenty* when she makes a decision you don't like! ("That dress makes you look frumpy." "This brand of dishwasher is too overpriced." "That carpeting is too dark.") Sometimes she insists you come along on her shopping trip because she intends to buy something for *you*. Surely you don't want her to bring home another lavender sport shirt, do you? Then, hey, go with her, keep her away from the unsavory options, and let her play dress-up with you.

You're her Ken doll, you know. Lucky you! The worst that can happen to you is looking better.

Think of your mother and you'll have to admit that just about every woman's world involves taking care of others, especially loved ones. And that includes you. But it's not just you. It's your children, too. So enter into her care-giving world by sharing parental responsibilities. (At least shoulder the tasks that don't make you throw up.) They're less unpleasant and more rewarding when done together. Read some books on effective fatherhood. Ask her to recommend a couple, and she'll eagerly get them for you. And pay particularly close attention to the section on kids in Chapter 10 of this book, "Common Pitfalls and How to Avoid Them."

3. Share Your World with Her.

Trust your woman to understand your work life, your leisure life, and your social life with other men. In fact, a lot of women are as into certain sports as you are. However, she might need more information about your world to be able to talk intelligently about it with you, so *explain* it to her. Tell her what you actually do all day—your routines, your special projects, and the characters you work and have lunch with. Offer to take her along with you to work, to visit your hangouts, and to watch your sporting activities. Even if she can't get away from her own job or other commitments, she'll be tickled with your offer.

Then let her be your friend, even your buddy. Confide your challenges, your concerns, and your insecurities in her. Once she understands your world, she might be able to help you negotiate it. She might have a different take on your boss's apparent moodiness, your team's internal conflicts, or your assistant's habitual forgetfulness. Remember a woman's interpersonal savvy and uncanny intuittion. Get them to work on your behalf. By the same token, you should celebrate your challenges and triumphs with her, too. The more she knows about your world, the more she can appreciate your successes – and admire you for them.

4. Listen to Her with Interest.

You've probably heard the term *active listening*, and this is definitely among the things that your woman wants you to do. In terms of your behavior, it means being able to paraphrase, in your own words – not mindlessly repeat – what she just said. Can you do that? In terms of your heart, active listening means empathizing with her, genuinely doing your best to understand what she is saying, and taking her opinions, feelings, and perceptions seriously. Yes, some of her perspectives may strike you as coming from another planet, no doubt Venus. But these give you the opportunity to make yourself shine by asking her to clarify her point and to give examples, *as long as* you ask with the earnest desire to understand, not with the irritated impatience to get the whole conversation over with. Then paraphrase her message back to her as accurately and empathetically as you. She will absolutely love you for this, guys! And her feelings will probably make more sense to you. If they don't, continue the discussion.

If you have no interest in what she has to say, you don't deserve her. What are you doing with her anyway?

Active listening prepares you to do well at the next sure-win way to keep your woman.

5. Talk with Her Openly and Often.

Be there for conversation with your woman. And I mean *really there* emotionally as well as physically. Good conversation is the life and breath, the super glue, of all relationships. It invigorates love long after passion dwindles.

Concerned about launching a meaningful conversation? Just check in with her regularly. Ask her how she feels and how she thinks about something, anything. Share your feelings and opinions, too – not just about your relationship but also about your job, your decisions, your dreams, hobbies, politics, food, the neighbors, the furniture, travel, clothes, a television show, the Internet – whatever crosses your or her path.

Where the finesse comes in is sensing when there's a problem in her mind between the two of you. The trick is to ask her what's bothering her *before* it builds up and she brings it up. Persist lovingly if she denies a problem or acts shy. For the subtle signals of trouble, see the Early Warning Signs of her leaving in Chapter 6. Like cancer, if you cut it out early enough, you can get it all and keep it from spreading.

Fighting fairly. No matter how much in love you and your woman are, you're eventually going to disagree about something. And sometimes, someone will get irritated, frustrated, or downright angry. The challenge is not to *avoid* conflict but to *manage* it, which means fighting fairly, so you don't let a bump on the tracks cause a major train wreck. How do you both fight fairly? Just follow a few ground rules:

• Listen actively to her point of view (see #4 above). Acknowledge it, and paraphrase back what you hear her saying. ("Okay, I think you thought that I was making fun of your cooking. Is that right? If it's not, correct me.") This shows that you're trying to get an accurate understanding of her perspective and that you accept it. Not that you necessarily agree, but you validate that she's telling the truth *as she sees it.* Never *assume* you know where she is coming from.

• When you express your point of view, start each statement with "I" (as above) to make it clear, even to a ticked-off woman, that you are talking *only* about your feelings, perceptions, and opinions. (Some pop psych books called it "claiming" or "owning" your own feelings.) In fact, I advise that you follow your "I" with a verb like "feel," "perceive," "believe," "think," or some other subjective word. This kind of phrasing leaves the other party with nothing to attack.

• Admit your mistakes, shortcomings, and contributions to the problem. It will inspire her to concede her own.

• Stick with the topic at hand. Don't load on other problems you've had with her to buttress your side. The extra weight will push the wedge between you deeper.

• Stop before a bomb goes off – that is, suspend your conversation if tempers start to flare. Physically work off the anger or let it subside before you pick up the conversation again.

• Look for resolution. Try to come to a common understanding of the conflict or problem, then ask what you can *both* do to resolve or solve it. Set a good example by saying what you're willing to do (or stop doing) first. You might want to start with some sort of compromise, but let her suggest solutions, too. Women tend to favor *resolving* a conflict when given a chance – a consequence of lower testosterone – so ask for her input. This will also win you love points.

• Forgive and be forgiven. The best way to earn your own forgiveness is to apologize, *not* for your point of view, but for anything you said that might have stirred up bad feelings between you. This will soften her heart, and she'll *have to* follow your heroic lead.

6. Take Pride in Yourself.

Do something really right – if not for yourself, then for your woman. One right thing you can do is to be a success at something – take of your pick of your job, a volunteer activity, a hobby, or an artistic endeavor – and without boasting, let her know you are. (Of course, some "special cases" of women, as described in Chapter 10, will be more demanding of success than others.) Your woman loves to see you shine, and she gets lots of status from it, too, especially with other women. If you want her to shine in your success just as brightly as you do, let her know how she helped you become successful. You know she did, and so does she.

Here's another thing that you'd better do right: taking care of your body. So if you're too bulky to be a Sumo wrestler or you look like you're pregnant with a six-pack, it's time to get active. Work out, pump iron, run, swim, walk, do yoga, learn a martial art, take up racket ball or tennis, sign up for an aerobics class, get into a team sport – just get moving in whatever you enjoy, or at least don't hate. Just pick something, anything you'll keep doing.

While you're at it, start watching your weight and trimming down your caloric intake. All that most men have to do is to start eating more home-cooked, non-fried food and avoiding fast food, bar food, and potato chips. This may mean becoming the head cook at home, given that so many women have rendered themselves helpless in the kitchen. And this definitely means eating breakfast at home and bringing your lunch with you to work. This life-style will not only make you thinner, especially when done in conjunction with exercise, but also make you richer. In a few months, you'll have more than enough money to pay for your health club membership.

Please note that I didn't ask you to give up beer or your favorite booze. They have plenty of calories, too, but I don't want to press my luck with you. You'd be wise, however, to switch to a light beer if you haven't already and to shop around for a lower-calorie mixer. Pour juices instead of sugary concoctions and choose the diet versions of sodas, ginger ale, and tonic water.

Your woman is likely to notice your weight loss before you do. Women are wired to weigh with their eyes.

7. Be Vulnerable.

Please, weed out of your mind all that male macho stuff you learned as a kid that vulnerability equates to weakness. Oh sure, that might apply in war when you're talking about *physical* vulnerabilities; remember Achilles and that troublesome heel of his? But the *opposite* is true when you're talking about a woman's perspective on *emotional* vulnerabilities. To women, vulnerability is incredibly appealing in a man. In fact, it's a virtue. An emotionally vulnerable man isn't afraid to feel finer emotions, to give up the tough male façade for a higher value, to really crawl out of his shell and care – and be more like her! Through a woman's eyes, vulnerability looks like courage. It conveys character and strength, as well as tenderness and trustworthiness. It *never* looks like weakness to her, and to be a liberated man means it doesn't to you either. *Quite* the contrary!

Be aware that emotional vulnerability is very hard to fake. Women look for it in a man's eyes. It expresses itself as a softness – you've heard of eyes like a puppy dog, right? – that belies a man's unspoken, but not immediate or desperate, fear that he could lose her and his major source of happiness. It's an acknowledgement of his emotional *need* for his woman. Women need to be needed, and nothing says needed like a little fear in a man's eyes.

If you hate hearing this, it's probably because you know that your fear of losing her gives her power over you. Yeah, and your point is? What do you think love is all about? It's a surrendering of power to the loved one. But it's mutual, so it's not like you're getting the short end of the wishbone. She needs you, too. And remember, the first sure-win way to keep your woman and keep her the way you love her is to trust her with your heart and be trustworthy with hers. With trust between you, your fear needn't turn to worry or suspicion.

One big "however": Just because your eyes may look like a puppy dog's doesn't mean you should *act* like a puppy dog. Please, no crawling to her on all fours, no tongue hanging out of your mouth, and no awkward fawning. Those behaviors indeed show weakness because they make a man look "needy." To a woman, there's a cavern of difference between a "man who needs her" and a "needy man." The latter is ... well, not quite a man. He's pitifully and desperately dependent on her for his sense of self-worth. Women have a word for him: "Yuk!"

8. Be Attentive.

Do you remember the way you treated your woman when you first found her and found love with her? What were you doing during your the first few months together, while you were getting to know her and wooing her. Remember how attentive you were? Oh, I hope you do! If you want to keep her as yours and just as lovable as back then, you've got to keep doing those things. And you thought you were off the hook now!

Okay, let me jog your memory. You opened doors for her, including the car door, which you also closed after she was comfortably seated. You *never* walked ahead of her, *never* let her carry a heavy load alone, and *never* criticized her driving. You *always* left her plenty of room in bed, *always* reminded her to wake you up if you started snoring, and *always* kissed her good-night. You also *always* noticed what she was wearing, what perfume she'd put on, and when she was having a good hair day, and you complimented her accordingly. In fact, you were *always* looking for little and big ways to show her that you loved her. Maybe it was making the coffee before she did, taking her car in for an oil change (or changing it yourself), or sewing a button on your shirt so she didn't have to. Maybe it was doing the laundry, going shopping with her, or – miracle of miracles! – changing the toilet paper roll.

Ah, it's all coming back to you now, isn't it? You were treating her with consideration and courtesy, regularly doing little favors for her, practicing little gallantries, and anticipating her everyday needs and desires. You were being "sensitive" and "aware." You were putting energy into her and the relationship. You were trying to please her. You were making her feel wanted.

Back then maybe you figured you had to do all that to win her heart. Then you won her heart and stopped doing it. You figured the job was done. Well, I'm here to tell you, *before it's too late,* that it's not. Remember the section, "The Falling Rate of Interest" in Chapter 1? A woman's work is never done, and a man's isn't either as far as his woman is concerned. She expects you to be the same man you were early in the relationship, and these are expectations that you yourself set up. Frustrate her expectations and you'll start seeing those telling signs of trouble I told you about in Chapters 5 and 6.

9. Be Romantic.

Being attentive is pleasing your woman at the basic level. It's just being consistent over time. It's Keeping Your Woman 101. If you really want to seal the deal, you'll want to take the more advanced course, 102, and step up from being attentive to being romantic, from making her feel wanted to making her feel "kept." What's being romantic? Go back to page 1 for some general ideas. Then ask your woman what she finds romantic. She'll love responding to that question! Just asking her is romantic in itself. Whatever she says, take mental notes and try out some of her suggestions.

Be well prepared to hear this facet of romance from your woman: never, ever, forgetting her birthday, Valentine's Day, or your and her anniversary. Then ask her, "Are there any other anniversaries that mean a lot to you, Sweetheart?" If you're savvy to some female fundamentals, you already know that some women want to celebrate quite a few with you, like the anniversaries of the day you met, the day of your first date, the day you said you loved her, the day you proposed, and God knows what other day. No matter how ridiculous these memorials may seem to you, put these days on your personal calendar the same way you do the Super Bowl. Then plan to do something to acknowledge them. You can give her a romantic card – yes, there are romantic greeting cards that celebrate nothing in particular but the love between the two of you – or just bring home a bottle of good wine. You don't even have to spend any money. Just put your arms around her and say (with conviction and a straight face, please), "Do you know what today is? (Of course she does, but tell her anyway.) It was eight years ago today that we first kissed." She'll richly reward you in food, sex, flattery – really whatever you want.

Your woman is also likely to consider expressions of love romantic. You can't go wrong with this basic: Reassure her with at least one "I love you" per day. It works like a nutritional supplement to keep the doctor away. Then sprinkle in generous numbers of thank-you's and compliments, including a few while making love. Beyond words, she may ask for more hugging, kissing, and physical play, maybe even public displays of affection as far as you both are comfortable. Chances are that her comfort point will be more advanced than yours. Quite a few women, especially older ones, are latent exhibitionists!

Speaking of sex, show passion in bed. Some women prefer it a bit rough, too, and your woman will tell you if she does. After all, she's not a China doll. But just as important as physical passion is that you show you care about her pleasure as well as your own. A truly great lover is someone who know – more accurately, *learns* – how to pleasure the other person. As you probably know by now, women don't go by set rules, so you have to ask her what turns her on.

Your woman may forget to mention some features of romance – surprise, for instance. Do you really want to sweep her off her feet? Then do something special for her out of the blue, on an otherwise ho-hum day. Bring her flowers, a love card, or a little gift. Do her a special favor. Take her out to dinner or for a drink. Ask her out on a date to see a boy-meets-girl movie (what you call a "chick flick"). Make her breakfast in bed one morning. Without getting too radical to start, suggest trying out a new sexual position or technique. As you'll read in the next chapter, injecting some innovation into love-making can help neutralize the debilitating effects of time and routine on a love relationship.

Another often overlooked component of romance is elegance – for example, an occasional dinner at a white-tablecloth-and-candle-light restaurant or a night out at the theatre or ballet. You may define "elegant" as "expensive," and it often is, but it doesn't have to be. For a woman, elegance has only two low-cost requirements: 1) You go to a beautiful place together, which can be a garden, a lake, an art show, a cute little town, or even a serene forest with a hiking trial. 2) You dress up for the occasion. You really resent that last requirement, don't you. Well, suck it up. There is nothing sexier to a woman than a man in a tux. This doesn't mean that you should don a three-piece suit to take a walk through a botanical garden (though she might just like that). But do dress at least a cut or two above your typical casual duds and put away the worn-out tee-shirt. If your woman craves turtlenecks (lots of women do), put one on. If the way you wear tight jeans turn her on, then pour yourself in a pair.

10. Act Like Her Favorite Actor.

Welcome to Keeping Your Woman 103. This is the frosting on your woman's cake, and it's oh so sweet to her! Are you ready to play the Big Time in the Theatre of Love?

Beyond attentiveness, beyond romance, lies fantasy. Every woman has a fantasy lover, a Prince Charming who lives only in her dreams. She doesn't expect to meet him, let alone settle down with him – at least not in this world. Still, she reserves the farthest depths of her heart for this phantom-man. As a rule, he resembles her favorite actor, be it George Clooney, Matt Damon, Brad Pitt, Ben Affleck, or Pinky Lee. She may have developed a picture of her fantasy man first and then found an actor who personified him, or she may have discovered her Prince in an actor. We are, of course, talking about the actor's public persona.

So what if you became like her favorite actor? She would *more* than love you. She would *adore* you. You'd really like that, wouldn't you?

Do you know who her favorite actor is? Well, you *should*. If you don't, you may not be ready for such an advanced curriculum as this one. You'll have to detour into a remedial course by *asking* her who her favorite actor is, and why. Note the "why." Her explanation will give you more general insight into what she idolizes in a man. Then you have some serious homework: to observe him. Rent the guy's movies, tape his television shows, or find pictures and videos of him on the Web. Then watch carefully how he projects those stellar qualities in the roles he plays. Study the way he talks, such as his accent and intonations, his verbal expressions, his smile, his stance, his walk, his gestures, the way he wears his hair, his clothes, and the way he looks at a woman. If he plays romantic roles, observe carefully how he wins a woman.

You are seeing exactly what your woman wants in a man, subtle traits and behaviors that she might never be able to articulate to you. Even if she could, she might not want to share her "ideal man" fantasy with you, because she wouldn't want to make you feel inadequate. But you should take heart in knowing that you must already have at least a few of those qualities, or you wouldn't have won her heart.

Your next assignment, should you choose to accept it, is to imitate the actor's appearance and behavior in as many ways and as well as you can. You can easily get a different haircut (show a picture of the actor to your hair dresser), buy a new shirt or pair of pants, speak a little differently, stand more this way or that way, and modify your facial expression when you look intently at your woman. You don't have to tell her what you're doing. Whether or not she figures it out, she'll love the style you're adopting. And that's all that matters to get an A in this course.

Congratulations! Now you know all the secrets of the universe – at least the universe of women. *You officially know what a woman wants.* And it wasn't so crazy, was it?

Chapter 10.

Common Pitfalls and How to Avoid Them

Okay, let's turn off the romantic violin concerto that accompanied the last chapter and get down into the gullies that trip relationships up. We'll look at ways to help pull you and your woman out. Don't cower. It'll be a lot more educational than depressing.

We all know – except when we're drugged on the first rush of a new allure – that even the strongest love is as fragile as a spider's web and probably stickier. It usually gets *harder*, not easier, to keep it healthy and halfway hot. After a while, life seems to *conspire* against your following the ways to keep your woman and against your being the man you and your woman really *want* to be. Ultimately the most frustrating thing is not knowing what's going wrong or what to do about it. Square the problem if she's complaining (and she probably is).

By the end of this chapter, you will know, as few men do. Not even many women do. Most lovers wander blindly through their amorous adventure like tipsy treasure hunters without a map. It's bad psychological hygiene. High schools ought to require a course like "How to Keep Love Alive in Spite of Life." But they don't.

Just *knowing* the pitfalls helps a lot. It may convince you to steer totally clear of some situations you'd just as soon not deal with. A few can be sidestepped. Or it can prepare you to expect certain predicaments so you don't react naively like an Oedipal little boy. Remember, that play was a tragedy.

We'll even go a step further and talk about the things you can *do*, and may *have to do*, to get through life's mine fields with your love intact. You can lead your woman through them, and become a genuine modern-day hero. Believe me, she'll notice and knight you.

Time

No couple lives happily ever after. Time is *not* on your side. It's a four-letter word. But then love is, too. So they fight it out.

Time can get the best of the best of us. We start out life with the unencumbered energy to bounce off walls – then, over the years, start to feel those walls closing in on us. We lose our limberness. Our wind winds down. Our reflexes grow reluctant. Our muscle melts into flab. In fact, *everything* on earth – buildings, cars, governments, baseball players – has a natural tendency to deteriorate over time. The issue is *how fast*?

You only have to look at the castles on the Rhine, Beijing's Forbidden City, a classic Packard, and Harrison Ford to see that a good thing can go on aging gracefully damn near forever. So can our bodies, if we treat them like the limited edition models they are. Time's destructive tendencies *can* be held in check. They only run amuck over what we neglect.

And so it is with love. It *doesn't* conquer all – not on its own, not if neglected and taken for granted. We have to *help* it conquer time. Or else.

How Time Lies, Cheats, and Steals. As the Good Book didn't exactly say, time giveth and time taketh away. Time giveth the stuff of trust, comfort, understanding, realism, patience, friendship, and synchronized rhythm. At least it can. But what it gives isn't *nearly* as inspiring as the stuff it can steal away: the energy to be your very best for one another; the spontaneity to cuddle in the kitchen; the romance to sip champagne between the sheets; the passion to pursue wherever possible; and mysteries between and within you to still be explored. If left to its "natural" let-the-flab-fall course, time *starves* love to *death*.

Just as in the physical world, there's entropy: Time runs energy down. It creates routine, cycles, predictabilities, inertia. You don't do anything *special* together anymore just because you don't do it *routinely*. Then you can't feel the *urge* to do it when you sense you *ought* to do it (like on a birthday or anniversary). Somehow you don't have much exciting to say to each other anymore. You feel you know each other's lives and thoughts too well. Or you don't know what to ask because you've lost track. Or you haven't cared quite enough to think about it.

You don't build dreams anymore. You don't share secret fantasies. You don't spin tales of your own private Camelot. You don't envision futures past Friday. You either assume them in silence or avoid thoughts of their coming.

You don't feel *driven* by love like you did. It's there (you believe), but it's not *compelling*. Not called to action. Not throbbing to express itself. So you unconsciously stop going out of your way to please her, to amuse her, or to entertain her. It's too much effort, and with uncertain results. You go your own way. You figure the feelings are mutual. And if things are stable, why bother?

"Why bother?" That's the guts of neglect. It's exactly what turns good people into idle bystanders of murders and rapes. It's the policy of crisis politics: Don't act until there's a catastrophe. It's a dreadful way to manage a situation.

It's easy to get neglectful because time is sneaky and dishonest. It creates the *illusion* that after a while together you and your woman have talked about every important issue, that there is nothing else to say. So you stop having *real* conversation. After all, you start to think if you haven't thought of anything *new* to talk about, you must have said it *all* – right? Wrong.

Time makes you believe that all the routines that you and your woman have are necessary, inevitable, satisfactory to all. Otherwise, they wouldn't be there – right? Wrong.

Time seduces you into domestic doldrums. It fools or frightens you into *feeling* settled, *being* settled. Even as your romantic urge eats away at your restless heart, you figure you're *supposed* to find happiness just having a place to come home to – right? Wrong.

Time even tells you that you can get away with getting careless. That you can be sloppy, crude, nasty, or dull, but it won't matter to your mate. That you can belch like a frat boy, sport a kangaroo belly, cavort around like a caveman, *and still* pique her passions – right? Wrong.

To triumph over time, you've got to blast through its bullshit, and *fight against it fast*. Only a damn fool would let love's fun and romance go to rot if he could keep them fresh.

How to Take on Time: I. Psyching up Exercises. The tactics that neutralize time boil down to the ways you can keep your woman and keep her the way you love her. But the real issue for you is how to get your mind *geared up* to do them sincerely, and *keep* doing them, *in spite of* time.

How to Keep Your Woman

Maybe you fear you can't anymore because you know your woman "a little too well" now. Or there've been too many dirty dishes, or silent nights, or nasty words between you. Or whatever once inspired you seems to have slipped away. I understand. That's the testiness of time. But, believe me, love's all in your mind.

Do you recall ever looking at weird black and white drawings that switch images on you? First, it's a Grecian vase; then it's two profiles facing each other? Or it's a lovely lady with a fancy hat one moment, and an ugly old lady's head the next? And remember when you're in a new apartment or house, how you're taken with the layout's twists and turns and nooks and crannies. Then after a while, when it stops surprising you, the place seems too simple and square?

When what you're *looking at* doesn't change but what you *see* does, you're getting a new "gestalt." It's like a different impresssion of what's real. And it's easy to forget how the first one looked, or felt, or sounded when you suddenly get a new one.

Now, try to remember how you saw your woman when you were first falling in love with her. It must have been the sexiest, most beautiful and fascinating gestalt that you had ever seen. Imperfections faded into the forgivable fringes. All you shared together stole center stage.

So what happened to that grand gestalt over time? Did you lose it to a less flattering one? Granted you were under the influence of love when your mind's eye feasted on it. But you weren't *crazy*, were you? And it's not like you didn't *know* her then, even though you may feel you know her better now.

In fact, maybe you know parts of her now even *less* well, especially those parts that made you pursue her. Remember her grace, her glowing warmth, her memorable smile, her purity of heart, her perceptive mind, her inspiring character? Has she really *changed*? Or are you forgetting to focus on *all* of her? Or forgetting how to bring out the *best* in her?

Oh, how quickly we forget the magic! We recall the *feeling* wistfully. But we forget the greatness in our lover that made it happen. Unless we're overwhelmed with it, it slips away from view. Your living-with-her gestalt of late may underplay it or even turn once-virtues into vices. Where you once saw her "spunk," you see her temper. What you once prized as her "guts," you fault as bitchiness. Her quick thinking mind now seems narrow and snappish. Her sensitive heart now looks overly so. After a few disappointments and domestic bouts, you've recast her in a maligning new light.

Want to get the magic back? Try this noble exercise. Let your mind wander back in time to that falling-in-love gestalt of her. Really *think* about it. Focus in on all the stellar qualities you saw in her at the time. If you're serious about this, write them down. Make a list. If you can't think of at least a dozen, you're either not trying or suffering from dementia. (Or perhaps you never really loved her to begin with.)

Okay, now go down the list and cross out any virtues you're *positive* that you were wrong about or that aren't there *at all* anymore. (You'll be unlucky to find two or three.) Now star the ones that you've come to see as somewhat detracting traits, and jot down what you see them as now.

Not to dismiss your less complimentary gestalt, as you've probably been down enough rocky roads with your woman to back it up. But isn't that glowing falling-in-love gestalt just the flip side? And isn't it still a real side of her, too? Can't you think of some recent times with you alone or with friends when she's shown her best side?

On to the next step: Give your woman half a chance. Cross out all those detracting twists of her traits. While you're doing that, recall a couple of nasty scenes that made you see her in these ways, and try to reinterpret her behavior more gently – if you can, as an outgrowth of her *virtues*. (If she was fighting with you for more independence, credit her courage, self-sufficiency, quest for growth, whatever.) Now, focus in on *all* of her stellar qualities, on your whole falling-in-love gestalt of her. And see her in your mind's eye *only in that enhancing light*.

Don't worry that you're leaving out part of the whole picture. Just try it. Give her that half a chance. Doesn't that feel better? Don't you feel a little rush of love's reverie again?

Hold the thought. And keep thinking it, at least a few moments every day. I *promise* you, that inspiring image of her will become more and more real each time. It's not silly hocus-pocus. It's reviving a lost horizon, a vision that got buried alive. It gives you a fuller and fairer view of your woman, an antidote to the dulling side effects of time and domestic life. And you'll start to treat her accordingly, more like the way you used to, more like a woman you really love. Then watch. People tend to act pretty much the way they think others see them. So your woman is likely to pick up your good vibes and, in turn, act more like that grand old gestalt. It's simple social psychology, and it works well on "normal" people (whoever they are, but your woman probably is among them).

Even so, you may need some help. Or you may want quicker results. Easy. *Tell her what you're doing.* That you feel time has taken its toll on both of you, so you've taken on this step-by-step "noble task" to refuel the old flames. And wouldn't she please help a little by parading her virtues (show her the list) as much as possible? Boy, will she be delighted! And will you ever get cooperation. Most women *love* to work on their relationships with their man. It'll be a piece of cake.

Want to make it even easier? Suggest that she try the same "noble task" on *her* image of *you*. You can't demand it. But you can remind her that love is a two-way street and conquering time is a two-person battle. You're just playing the heroic leader who starts the war. Chances are she'll be amenable, if not downright enthusiastic, to recast her image of you in a more enhancing light.

How to Take on Time: II. The Call to Arms. There's just one more step, and if you're following the others sincerely and staunchly, this one will flow pretty naturally: *Start breaking those time-rutted routines,* especially the ones you both like the least. *Try doing some new and different things*, including those things you used to do more when you were falling in love.

Stop acting like "her ol' man" and treating her like "your ol' lady." Try thinking of your evenings together as "dates" – one of you inviting the other over for dinner – and your weekends as days to "steal away" or "shack up." Don't let a few household chores discourage you. Why *shouldn't* you think of your woman as a date? She would be to any other man. *He'd* be a real gentleman to her. *He'd* put on his most appealing persona. You should, too.

Start with the little things. Dress a little more nicely for dinner. Put on a nice, clean Oxford shirt instead of your ratty old college tank top. Make her and yourself a pretty-looking drink to relax with. You can find pre-fab mixes for the fanciest concoctions. Compliment her on her cuisine. Or take her out for a drink or dinner more often. Pick places where you dress up a bit. Ask her out first a few days before, as you would a date. At least once make the call for the sitter yourself.

Nothing numbs love like the sound of silence. So have something to *tell* her every night: a little intrigue from work, a tidbit in the news, your weird dream last night, any new thought on *anything*. Then when you've talked about that, have something to *ask* her, and not just how her day went. Follow up on a story she's shared before. ("How did that new guy you work with solve his conflict with his boss?") Or ask how she feels about something: her cousin's divorce, the novel she's reading, or the new wallpaper in the dining room. Or revive some getting-to-know-you topics. After all, there are parts that you haven't shared. And besides that, people change. So probe some values and beliefs together. Swap a few more childhood memories. Chat about your latest hopes and dreams or the lessons in life you've learned lately.

Have some fun together every day. Dust off the guitar. Get out some old board games. Take up a foreign language or hobby together. Plan a party or a trip. Drop in on friends. Put photos in an album. Go bowling. Play miniature golf. Put together a picnic lunch. Take in a movie, a concert, or a play. Roam through an art gallery, a museum, or a shopping mall. Check out a swap meet, a night club, or a local fair. Challenge a nature trail, a water slide, or a roller coaster. Mini-vacation for a weekend near home. Cook some wild gastronomic delight together. Try *anything* you'd both enjoy and don't do all the time. All it takes is *one* of you to come up with ideas. If *you* start, she'll get inspired soon enough.

Now, on to the biggest things – well, one in particular: sex, of course. We dig our deepest ruts in bed. We tend to stick with old reliables that guarantee to get us off. "There is no *bad* sex," we say. So we stagnate – scared to break stride and try making it better, or even *discuss* it. But we *have* to, or our libidos will lay down and die. Of course, the longer you've run a bedroom routine, the tougher it is to break it. It might even arouse strange suspicions, you fear. But there're ways to get past the road blocks of time.

Check out a tasteful sex manual, like Alex Comfort's *The Joy of Sex*. It must be in its umpteenth edition by now. And ask yourself what you haven't been doing that you'd really like to try. Don't be too quick to conclude that your woman won't do it or that you could only do it with anyone but her.

Suggest a couple of your passionate proposals (not twenty at once, please) in a private place where you usually *don't* make love. Avoid your rut-worn bed. Bring them up when you're cuddling by the fire, or laying out on the lawn, or relaxing in a hotel room. Or after enticing her into your bubble bath or shower. Now you've got a *context* for testing out new territory. And you're conveniently located near places to try it. Then if you follow up with inquiries on what *she'd* like to venture, you won't have to stammer out so many suggestions yourself.

Give each novel notion at least a couple of tries. (Even the most simple sex wasn't great the first time, right?) But don't feel you have to invent a new technology every time. Novelty should be kept novel. It should vary and enrich good routines, not become one. And it should free both your spirits into fantasy, not strap them to a script or a standard.

You see, love is no different from you. It can stay young and virile for years. But only if it *thinks* uninhibitedly young and *executes* moderately mature. It needs playful self-expression, vigorous workouts, and a balanced variety of delights to feed on.

Kids

No matter how endearing and adorable, they're as hard on a couple's love as they are on furniture and clothing. Unless you have some yourself, it's easy to dismiss the trade-offs they involve because people have been having kids for millions of years (usually without thinking about it), and most of us still do. Then there are all kinds of soppy-eyed romantic notions surrounding motherhood, fatherhood, baby's first smile, the pitter-patter-of-little-feet, and watching your kid graduate from college.

During the past decade or two, Society has been pushing parenthood on younger generations with more advertising, television shows, and movies aimed at families. It's the same kind of trend-fabricating promotion that the U.S. government and mass media executed in the late 1940s and 1950s to generate the post-war baby boom. After all, children cost a lot of money, so they're good for the economy.

Not to come on too cynically, but parenthood isn't for everyone. And thank God, nowadays we have a choice. It's okay *not* to have kids, more okay than it is not to drink in some circles. It's also okay to *have* one or two, but only if you *both* want them and value family life over sex and romance. It's downright *stupid* to have them "to save the relationship" (they can kill it), or to flatter your ego (they might be monsters), or "to take care of you later" (they probably won't), or just because "she wants them" (the days of absentee fatherhood are over). Kids involve a much bigger commitment than you'll ever make to any woman or man. Parenthood is forever, and you have to take what you get.

Of course, if you've already contributed to the gene pool, you know what I'm talking about first hand. What you may *not* know is how *normal* your misgivings and adjustment problems are and how you can cut your losses on the love front.

First, let's separate fact from fairy tale. A couple of decades ago, an advice-to-the-lovelorn column reported the results of a survey that over 70% wished they weren't. They said that the kids cost them more freedom and trouble than they were worth. Not that their views represented those of the nation or of any other particular group. The columnist had just invited readers with children to drop her a line, and a lot of unhappy parents seized the chance to vent their regrets.

My interviews don't represent world opinion either. But most of the parents I talked to weren't enthralled with the role either, whether they had toddlers or teenagers. Those with grown children were typically glad the job was over, and the women especially recalled years of depression and self-denial. The few who really got off on it had chosen parenthood for the *right* reasons and had young school-age kids who could talk and play maturely and hadn't started lipping off yet.

Still, everyone had something good to say about children. They give you insight into yourself. They allow you to relive your own childhood and make a lot more retrospective sense of it. They're often funny and fun to play with. They connect you socially with other parents and the local community. They offer a chance to express, extend, and, of course, regenerate yourself. They *can* bring you and your woman together in a major common project, at least as long as you share similar child-raising values. (Heaven help you if you don't.) And when they come down with the mumps and you have to cancel your vacation, or you're both dying to go out together and you can't find a babysitter, they can bring you together in bearing a common burden, as well as learning advanced lessons in love and patience.

When you look at national surveys (the kind the government calls "Quality of Life"), most parents say that they're "pleased" or "delighted" having children in general. But they do have a laundry list of complaints when they're asked about specifics. Typically near the top is the effect on the marriage. In fact, you can chart the standard rise and fall of marital happiness over time. It starts out as high as a kite and drops like a dumbbell with the birth of First Baby. Then it doesn't really recover – if the marriage lasts so long – until after the last child leaves the house. Of course, children usually make *family* life happier, but that's different from *marital*. And depending upon your priorities, *life* happiness may either wax or wane.

Life Just Before and After Baby. So what usually happens between you and your woman when baby makes three? Well, it starts just weeks after one of your sperm scores. Her whole hormonal system clicks into a baby-producing mode. And for the first three months, she may feel as sick as a Legionnaire and as sexed up as a spayed bitch. Food tastes funny and booze repulsive. She's always nodding out or running off to the john. She feels feverish and nauseous, like she's got a nasty flu. It's enough to make you doubt that there's *any* connection between sex and babies.

Later on, she starts feeling better. But she may come down with backaches and other bothersome body kinks – some of which you may actually feel *yourself*. All this tends to make a future father feel mighty protective. You become gallantly attentive to your woman's needs, nobly helpful around the house, and eager to punch out anyone who so much as bumps into her on the street.

But a father-to-be is also prone to act like a baby himself at times. After weeks of laundry duty, you may suddenly go running to your woman asking how to turn on the washer. Why? Because you need a lot of extra reassurance now. You need to know you'll still be first and foremost in her heart after Squiggums comes along. And it doesn't seem noble to outright *ask* her. So instead you succumb to bouts of helplessness.

Actually your fears are well founded. Many if not most men *do* lose their place of honor to the kids they spawn. Lots of women get off on motherhood more than they do on you. And some (maybe more) marry mostly to have a family. You're a key part of it, to be sure, as father and provider. But the children are the centerpiece. And as *husband*, you're just background.

Of course, this is only bad news if you're *not* so family-focused and your woman *is*. But most of you men aren't, at least not initially. Almost all of the dads I talked to felt left out, even shut out, by the new mother-child coalition. More active fathers felt it less, and their new bundles of joy won them over in a few months or years. But it's seldom an easy time for men. Their love-life happiness hits all-time lows, dipping even below women's, which is otherwise *always* lower. Once again, you men prove to be the true romantics of the species.

To make your love-sharing adjustment harder, your sex life continues to suffer. And this is especially rough on *you* because you men really rely on sex – more so than women – to express your love and be reassured of hers. Sex is your *language*, and you get muzzled for a while.

Even after the easiest births, obstetricians usually forbid intercourse for six weeks. And after trickier ones, the ban can go weeks longer. Some women feel enough lingering discomfort to not get off for months. There are, of course, other ways to make love. But they just don't tend to materialize. Even after a year, couples do a lot less touching, holding, necking, and pillowing of all kinds. Not surprisingly, they don't *feel* as close as they used to, either. In time – possibly a long time if more kids come along quickly – the mating rate returns to normal. But even so, men often complain it's not quite enough.

Married with Children. The brown-out in the bedroom only reflects currents of change throughout the household. Babies need constant care, toddlers constant chasing after, and older kids constant attention and guidance. As one bothered father put it, "They are a constant presence." Parenthood is emotionally exhausting and physically fatiguing. It leaves a lot less energy for romantic romps – and a lot less room. A child takes over the entire house, especially wherever you happen to be. Parenthood also leaves a lot less time for anything else. Your activities change to include and amuse Junior. So you spend Saturday at Kiddyland instead of an art fair. You catch more Disney flicks than sexy French imports. You dine out at six under orange fluorescence instead of after eight in candlelit class. In fact, you're more likely to stay home all evening and watch your kid's favorite TV shows. Forget the spontaneous jaunts with your woman to go dancing, or to drop in on friends, or to take a moonlit walk. What if Junior wakes up crying? And you can't stay up late when he's up at 5:30 in the morning and it's your turn to wash, dress, and feed him.

Parenting so dominates every day that it's no wonder couples lose track of each other. They're tending so much to their child that they let their own loving fall by the wayside. They start calling each other "Mom" and "Dad," and actually *seeing* each other that way. Their own conversation turns into baby talk or revolves around Junior's potty progress. They let anniversaries slip by without fanfare. They don't take the time to look their best for each other.

Which brings us to what I call the Motherhood Mousy Trap. It's a syndrome that falls under "Going to Seed." It can stem from Security Slippage, Living-the-Dream Letdown, or Biting-the-Bullet Blues. (Thumb back through Chapter 5.) But the symptoms are pretty much the same. A woman's attention turns totally to the child and to whatever makes her mothering tasks easier. So she stops wearing make-up. She gets an asexual wash-and-wear hair cut. She starts living in middle-age housecoats and drool-stained shirts, or never gets out of maternity clothes. In addition to carrying a baby around, she's carrying a bundle of extra weight. She's not that much fun to be with either. She's too busy, too tired, and not too interested in much except Baby anymore.

At the same time, a new dad may start running the Fatherhood Rat Race. He's so into playing the provider role, into securing his expanding kingdom, that he starts striving to bring in more money while ignoring the people he's doing it *for*. Often he feels insecure himself, especially of his monetary manhood. Sometimes he just wants to escape from the kid-raising chaos of his castle. Whatever the reason, he loses touch with the fortress he's trying to fortify and the lady he leaves in waiting.

All of this doesn't happen to *all* parents, or it happens to a lesser degree. But some drifting apart is inevitable, and the wedge gets driven deeper when a second kid comes along.

Yes, I said some lovers' languor is *inevitable*. But you can prevent the worst or retrieve some losses by knowing the pitfalls of parenthood, as you do now, and taking care to avoid stepping in them.

First, if it's not too late, make the decision about having kids *very carefully*. You don't owe it to Society or your parents to have them. Many couples choose not to and never regret it. So neither your good name nor your social life will suffer. Don't think you can just let *her* have them and raise them. Things *never* work out like that. Besides, *she'll* be into motherhood and will drift away from you even further. If you and your woman reach an impasse, it's the most blessed reason under heaven to break up. (See Chapter 13, "When to Let Go.")

Then if the two of you agree on good grounds to take the plunge into parenthood, fine. Just don't forget to agree to tend to your loverhood, too. When she's pregnant (and not feeling sick), act as passionate as you know how. Get off on her juicier tits and tummy. Make her feel like a sexy Madonna. Let her know *in words* if you feel insecure, and she'll no doubt reassure you. At the same time, face the fact like a man that you *chose* to make room for another on your throne. And who could be more worthy than your very own child? Besides, you'll be gaining an admirer.

Don't dodge daddyhood. Be as active as your time allows and you won't feel left out. Just budget in a Lovers' Allotment of time as well. As soon as Baby can go three or four hours without a dire need, seize the time for you and your woman, at least a couple of blocks of time per week. Blow the bucks on a babysitter, beg or bribe a relative, or time trade with other parents. But *be together*, just the two of you. Talk and have fun as *lovers*. It doesn't matter much *what* you do, as long as you don't dwell on Junior. If you can't afford or don't feel like a night on the town, steal away on a picnic or just park in the sticks. Or you can even stay home in the most remote room and play games and get silly on wine. Or act out a sexual fantasy or two. The best things in life come cheap, if not free.

A few little don'ts mean a lot, too. *Don't* let any wedding or bedding anniversary pass by unnoticed. Exchange cards, gifts, and kisses, and celebrate in style. Ditto for each other's birthdays. Don't save the festivities just for your kids. And *don't* call one another "Mom" and "Dad." You don't go to bed with your mother, do you?

You're *lovers*, remember? Even if you're legal. So remind each other regularly by staying on a first-name or pet-name basis.

Double Careers

Double careers are a double-edge sword. They can double the closeness between you and your woman. After all, you're both bucking the same bullshit out there and can plot your power plays together. In addition, you may respect her more, and she can appreciate your problems better. She leans on you less to fulfill her ambitions, and you dump on her less about piled-up dishes and over-priced dresses.

Of course, you both have more money to play with, though double careers may or may not double it. Your woman probably pulls in less dough than you do. And if you have a tot or two, you may put out hundreds or thousands of dollars in child care each year. Not to mention the higher commuting costs and annual dues to Uncle Sam. Still, your woman's job may be essential to her health and happiness and to your household's economic well-being. You're just going to have to hammer out some agreements on some issues.

Housework. Remember my telling you in Chapter 2 about the typical overwrought working wife whose hubby refuses to help? Well, to hell with all of you men who won't, or who won't instead buy her some help. If your woman's too harried to give you the quality company you want, you're getting what you deserve. You know, housework isn't so horrible if you do it together as a team. And if you halve her time for housework, you can double her time for *you*. But, please, don't require grandiose displays of gratitude. Do you send *her* flowers for scrubbing the floor and serving dinner?

Money. Unless one of you is allergic to handling money, both of you have a right to manage your own *on* your own, as well as common funds together. It may take a bit of creative accounting, but you can set up a system to make it easy. Trade in joint checking for separate accounts. Just keep each other's names on both for legalistic ease. This way you won't waste valuable time together squaring a checkbook or arguing over who's spending for what. (Remember, as Mama used to say, what you don't know won't hurt you.)

Then you both need to work out a plan for paying your common expenses: rent or mortgage payments, utilities, food, child expenses, household items, and insurance – along with a good-time slush fund for joint travel, entertainment, leisure, party-throwing, gift-giving, and hell-raising. You may want to set up a third communal account that you both contribute to monthly. Or just routinely divide the bills and the budgeted expenses between you. Either way, make the system *equitable* – from each according to your paychecks. So if you take home one-third more than she does, you pay one-third more of the common costs. It's only fair. If there are funds left over in your communal account, it would be most gracious to split them evenly between you or to tuck them away in joint savings.

Naturally, if one of you makes *much* bigger bucks, the better-padded pocketbook has to pay far more. After all, if you're dragging in a Mercedes salary and she's not, you wouldn't want to keep her in an old beat-up VW life style. (Besides, you probably couldn't keep her at all.) So whatever she needs to have to complement your status (like diamond-studded duds), you pick up the tab for and whatever you give her (like a Porsche), you pay for to maintain.

Time. Both your calendars full of appointments? Don't forget to schedule time *together*, and keep them. I mean it. Dumb, you say? After all, you come home every night eventually. Sure, but just to wind down, like a dragged out rat from a tread-wheel race.

But you Careerists are always up for appointments – from the top of the morning to the rear end of the evening. You psyche yourself up for them. In fact, without one, you may go limp. Okay, use the same technique for quality time with your woman. Schedule a couple of evenings or afternoons a week to be your *best* together. Pencil them in your appointment book so you can psyche yourself up in advance. *Plan* something relaxing to do, even if you're staying home. Then woo your woman with all the style you'd give your most important client. And isn't she?

Transfer, Move, and Separations. Double-career couples pray that they don't have to face this worst-fear phenomenon. Yet sooner or later, many of them have to. It goes with today's territory – an oddly compatible combo of women's new work ambitions and a mighty high cost of living. It's rough terrain for relationships.

Actually you have several options for dealing with the problem. It's just that they vary from lousy to dreadful. Consider your and your woman's career values and contingencies, and pick the least lousy for both of you.

"She Always Goes (or Stays) with Me." Not necessarily bad if she's not concerned with career advancement, or has little chance for it, or has skills in demand almost anywhere (for example, nursing). Otherwise, her career suffers, and she'll get depressed getting moved around like furniture. Always gain full support before you decide on a move, or you may wind up moving alone.

"I Always Go (or Stay) with Her." Ditto, ditto, ditto for you.

"We Alternate Going with Each Other." Not bad if you're both willing to detour downward on your way up. Whoever's turn it is to play prime mover may still have to compromise on relocations to keep the other's career alive. I knew a fast ladder-climber in the paper industry who kept taking transfers to rustic lumber hamlets – not exactly pockets of opportunity for his public relations wife. By the time they got to Poulsbo, WA, she divorced him.

"We Go Wherever the Bigger Paycheck Is Promised." Several possible pitfalls: The bigger paycheck may be eaten up by a higher cost of living or by a drop in the other's earning capacity. Once you opt for this arrangement, it's likely that the same one of you will *always* be getting the bigger paycheck, so it could quickly degenerate into one of you always going (or staying) with the other.

"Darling, I'll Join You as Soon as I Can." Just dandy if one of you has a *realistic* chance of arranging a comparable move and just needs a little time. And if you can afford to support two households for a while. And as long as the separation doesn't drag on (see below). Can be logistically messy with kids.

"We'll See Each Other Whenever We Can." In other words, you each go your separate career ways and plan to rendezvous on weekends or whenever, *indefinitely*. Expensive, of course, between

two households and transportation costs. Messy to unfeasible with kids. Terrific for both careers. (All those free evenings to work!) Terrible for most relationships. Worse than terrible the longer the separations and the shorter the times together. Even the most intimacy-intended couples lose the symphonic rhythm of their daily routines. The little details of life slip by without sharing. Then bigger ones. Reunions shift from celebrations to conferences of coordination. ("Our car insurance went up last month. Do you think you can cover the difference? After all, I'm covering the credit card bills.") The distance and difficulties may endure until somebody finds a Somebody Else to share delights on a more daily basis. Not that this *need* end the relationship; it only *usually* does.

Pretty bleak picture? Well, I'm just telling you what I've seen and heard. One woman I talked to waited three years to get a two-thousand-mile transfer to rejoin her husband – just in time to put a kink in his plans to run off with a Somebody Else. As it turned out, her timely move saved the marriage, but it took two pain-packed years to get it back on track. One has to wonder if the result was worth it.

Another couple survived a different variation on the theme for ten years. The woman had a flexible enough job to split her week equally between her workplace and her home with hubby a quick flight away. An ideal arrangement for keeping a marriage romantic? It was for a while. Then her split week evolved into a double life – two homes, two sets of friends, two life styles – one of which her husband shared no part in. In time, predictably, there were two men. As I said, the couple survived, but maybe just because the Right Other Man didn't come along.

In fact, only one case I know of worked out really well: two high-powered professionals who married in middle age and lived on separate *continents*. But that's the way they *courted*, too. Frankly, they'd been single for so long that they shared no urge to merge lives.

The moral of the story *isn't* to *avoid* the committed Career Woman. She can be the most stimulating and least whiney type to live with and the most understanding of *your* workaday world. Not to mention the bucks she brings in and the freedom she may give *you* to change careers or chase a rainbow. Just bear in mind you've got a balancing act, and you can't expect her to do all the juggling alone.

In-Laws

The solutions to this problem are pretty simple. No doubt you've heard them say, when you marry, you marry your mate's whole family, and don't think it's different if you're only shacking up. If your in-laws or *hers* (that's your family, Mac) are a meddlesome burden – if they cause tensions between you or drain your time – here are a few simple rules for getting them off your backs:

1. Be independent. *Never* take money, jobs, "deals," or any big favors from them. Don't owe them *anything*.

2. Be inconvenient. Live far enough away from them that frequent visiting costs too much time or money. Moving across town in a big metropolitan maze like Boston or the Los Angeles area may deter them as effectively as changing states.

3. Be busy. Have other plans for holidays. Spend Christmas in the Caribbean. Visit old friends or other relatives you like. Or proclaim some days sacred for the two of you.

4. Be diplomatic. Listen to your in-law's advice – you owe them that – but don't feel obligated to take it; you're not. If you don't and they gripe, reassure them you didn't ignore it. (Occasionally you really shouldn't.)

5. Then, be great to them. When they're out of your hair, you'll find room in your heart. Aging parents especially need your love more than you need theirs. Call them sometimes before they call you. Give them gifts they'll enjoy, like a subscription to *Senior Living*. Send them family photos. Write them thank you notes, even for the tablecloth you can't use and the tie you'll dare wear only once for them. Let little disagreements slide by with a nod, and shift topics when you feel big ones coming.

Pity the eager, young union organizer I interviewed who brought his work home to his mother-in-law, a well-heeled widow with right-to-work views. His woman got caught in the middle, pushed from both sides to choose between Mother and her man. Then guess who she figured would be tougher to replace....

Other Woman (Ex's and Extra's)

If you're one of the many men who have more than one woman in your life – either left over from the past or on the side for *any* purpose – you'd better sharpen your managerial skills. You have a situation to *manage*, no matter how innocent the Other Involvement(s) may be.

It's stupid to let it ride till a problem arises. If you do, one will. And it's ugly business picking thorns out of your side, then trying to earn back your woman's trust – or your woman herself. It's so much easier if you watch your step and don't stumble into a briar patch to begin with. And you wind up a lot freer to fraternize with other females.

Jealously is like booze. A little of it is healthy, fun, enlivening. When you and your woman are aware that you're both attractive to the opposite sex, it keeps you on your toes. You don't take each other for granted. A touch more jealousy on occasion may even stimulate a sporting competitive spirit. But past a certain point, you start to lose your balance. You can't see straight. You act crazy. You pull back in paranoia one moment and lash out in rage the next, neither of which helps your cause. You want to make your woman's cheatin' heart bleeds as much as you want to win it back. Meanwhile, yours is breaking.

No wonder writers from passion-pulp-novelists to Marcel Proust spike so many stories with jealousy. It makes great copy. Characters can do *anything* under its spell. And so can real people.

In fact, you fellows can flip out worse than women. Lots of you get *violent*. Smashing furniture. Beating your wives. Killing yourselves softly with liquor. Then punching each other out – and worse. Jealous *women* are relative pussycats. They just fall apart, scream like banshees, and kick you out of the bedroom. They *rarely* ruin your business, destroy your name, and murder, like on TV. Of course, if pushed, they'll leave you and take your children with them. So it's not like they have nothing on you.

I can't cite a string of studies, but my impression is that women on the whole are a bit less prone to jealousy than you are to begin with. And it's not because they don't catch your drift toward other women. We've already established they're more attuned to the subtlest social cues. (I've known only one strange exception who couldn't see her hubby's full-blown love affair going on right under her nose.) And it's not because they don't believe you roam. Almost every woman knows the stats by heart: that half of you married men get it elsewhere at one time or another, and that's almost *twice* the percentage of married women who do.

No, if anything, their knowing that you're prone to roam makes them *more tolerant* of you. Besides, you usually do it for such *innocently crude* reasons in women's eyes: to satisfy your curiosity (how different did you *think* it would feel?); to manifest your manhood (really now!); to meet a physical need (understandable if it's been a while); to get womanly warmth (it's wiser to try to fix things up with your woman); to pull off a fast-lane pass (whatever salvages your self-image); to reinvigorate your libido (just bring the energy back home); or to express a flattering fondness for a female friend (safe within rigid limits).

The point is, you seldom do it for love, *real love,* as though your lifetime allegiance is shifting. That's more the way of women. Their infidelity is straight from the heart – serious stuff. When it comes to the lighter diversions – like the desires that drive you to cheat – most of them are content just to flirt.

Women are also less possessive than you. Not only are they used to your "taking" your freedom, but they don't much believe in trying to "own" someone else. (Remember who led the Abolitionist Movement?) That's why they talk and rebel so much when you make them account for their time. Those who tend toward possessiveness typically express it as overbearing mothers.

Of course, some women are more jealous than others, and it's not just "the insecure." Some of the most inadequate-feeling women are the *most* willing to let you wander. What better way to keep you coming home than to let you leave for a while? It's a sad strategy to be sure, often settled upon by women who feel they've gone to seed, never bloomed, been cursed with veggie brains, or otherwise lack the magic to keep a man.

On the other extreme, atypical types like the Adventuresome Women (see Chapters 4 and 11) may *issue* you a hunting license (and themselves as well). It's not that they don't care. They're just gambling, as is normal for them, on your unassailable attraction to their exotic allure. They figure you won't find better, so they can afford your fooling around. If they turn out to be wrong about you, then *you* must have been about yourself as well. Not that their hearts don't bleed, too, especially over their *own* shortfall in foresight.

So it's the vast array of women in the middle to look out for. And chances are that your woman falls somewhere in this relatively jealous-prone middle who don't take your roaming so lightly. So pay attention! We're going to cover the equally vast array of Other-Woman relationships and look at how to prevent them from causing you trouble. But first, let's look at the two Basic Laws of Female Jealousy:

Law 1. Women get jealous of your energy and where you're putting it -- not so much your abstract "love" or precious fluids. Your energy takes many concrete forms in their eyes, and they keep careful watch over where it's going and where it isn't.

Remember "Standard Weights and Measures" way back in Chapter 1? Okay, let's review the fundamentals. Women define and operationalize "your love" much more complexly and concretely than you do, and than you do *her* love as a rule. It's not just no-looming-problems-between-you and not just your avoiding some obvious no-no's. It's affirmative actions across a dazzling variety of contexts. For a woman, then, love is like money, a highly liquid and transferable medium of exchange. It should, therefore, "transfer" into you giving her your highest quality time and attention, your most lavish material outlays, your liveliest libido, and exclusive entrée into your most private world. So if she sees or senses that some Other Woman is getting the best or most from you in *any* way, her plasma will turn to poison.

Law 2. The antidote to jealousy is reassurance. In fact, its prophylactic properties are quite amazing. Keeping your woman reassured can let you get away with mild forms of murder. Now, this may sound simple enough, but it isn't. You men don't know *how* to give reassurance very artfully and rarely give enough, especially when it's needed. Or more accurately, you lose your touch after that first frenzied phase of infatuation.

How do you reassure your woman? Word and deed, of course. But a very special, potent brew to ward off jealousy. You have to spice up your I-love-you's with some reasons why, including why you love her *more* than the Other Woman in question. It may sound like catty business making these comparisons. And if your O.W. relationship is as pure as the driven snow, it may seem like a belaboring of the unnecessary. But you have to understand that women draw comparisons with potential heart-robbers all the time – the same way you do among yourselves when it comes to net worth and athletic prowess. And if anything, women *overestimate* one another's allure. So administering the medicine I'm prescribing may make *you* nauseous, but it'll feel very soothing to *her*.

Think *specific* and as *honestly* as possible, or you won't pull it off). Tell your woman that you find her *much more* intriguing, intelligent, sensitive, sexy, attractive, trustworthy (check all that apply) than Suzy Suspicious at the office. You don't have to say anything insulting about Suzy. Just put your woman on the highest pedestal.

The follow-up in deed follows the same ideas: Give her and *only* her all those bests and mosts of your energy, intimacy, masculinity, and liquidity. Not that you shouldn't give *some* to *some* Other Women *some*times. But *your* woman has to feel she's primo on your list of recipients.

Notice I said that she has to *feel* primo. "Objective reality" isn't the issue. Maybe she *is* primo to you but *thinks* some Other Woman is getting the best of your whatever. If so, you've got to convince her that she's off base. How? 1) Tell her she is (lovingly, of course – not like her head is up her taco). 2) Back your case up with specific examples of how you've given her more of your whatever than you've given to Ms. Whomever. 3) Give her a little extra whatever until her dark cloud blows over. And it will if you're convincing.

Then again, maybe she's got *good reason* to suspect that some Other Woman is getting the better of you. She may notice how lost in conversation you get with Samantha Smarts. Or how your tongue hangs out and your tail wags when you're around Vicky Vivacious. Or that your mind seems to be light years away when you're around her, and she wonders who it's on.

Far be it from me to recommend that you give your Other Women up. Why should any of us expect only one member of the opposite sex to fulfill all our needs and desires forever? (Silly, isn't it?) Besides, you don't *have* to give anyone up – not if you're willing to do Double Duty. That is, you can talk, flirt, or fool around with any Other Woman you want *as long as* you do it with *your* woman, too, and do it with the same enthusiasm. Okay, it's not always possible. But the point is to try to approximate the same high-quality contact with your woman. The more brightly you can shine with each other, the less she'll mind the glow you give off around the Other Woman.

Now that you know the basics, let's dig down into the specific pits that you men fall into with your Ex's and Extra's, and how to stay above ground with your Present Primary.

Your Ex (If You Have One or More)

You figure you're through with her, with no detectable desire to go back. But then again you don't *hate* her either. You can even recall things you *like* about her. You may see her occasionally on a cordial basis: to pick up and drop off kids, to settle business, and perhaps to swap triumphs and tribulations. If you're not quite friends, you share a distant family tie that no other woman or man can put asunder. So you're slightly dumbfounded when your current woman shows concern.

Don't be. Remember that women think *comparatively*, and they project that you do, too. *And you do*. You just don't put the time and complexity into it that they do or that they *think* you do. So your woman is primed to worry about how she measures up to your earlier *objet(s) d'amour*, whether in cooking, copulating, conversing, or captivating the people you want to impress. She'd like to be the *best* in everything. So what if she senses she's not surpassing every other woman in your past.

Well, maybe you've told her a few historical tidbits that would have been better left unsaid. (Maybe you couldn't have known her sensitive spots at the time. For future reference, keep your mouth shut until you do.) Or maybe she fears that funny family tie with your ex could turn incestuous. So head her off at the pass and tell her it can't. Or maybe you're giving your ex some precious commodities that your current wasn't eager to share. So give your former a little less and your current a little more.

A best-intentioned guy I know named Nat got into hot water with his second wife for trying to get his first one out of it. He felt a not-so-strange sense of duty to his ex because she hadn't done so well since their split. She'd hooked up with a jerk, had his baby, paid his bills, and shared his frustrations and failures. Meanwhile, Nat had done mighty well financially and emotionally with Number 2. So he felt it only right to share his wealth with the less fortunate: first, hand-holding, tear-drying, and homespun therapy; than manly help around her house; then money. (He also had a little guilt to work out.) But from the therapy stage on, Number 2 started calling foul. *She* needed some of his homespun therapy herself, and Nat was oiling only the squeakier wheel. He was neglecting tasks around *their own* home, then giving away money that was as much *hers* as his. And *she* didn't have a penny's worth of love or guilt toward Number 1.

If the moral of this all-too-true story isn't all too obvious: *Don't* render services to an ex at the cost of your current. In other words, you've got to do Double Duty if you choose to ex-tend yourself. And *don't* give money beyond your contractual obligations. It's not all *your* money to give. If it's a little extra for your kids, ask your woman's permission *first*, not her absolution *after*. *Do* tell her all the ways she surpasses your long-left love(s) – not just once during those early true confessions, but again and again (without mentioning names). She wants to be your *very best*.

Innocent Extras: Your Female Friends

You're on absolutely solid ground claiming a right to share chummy interests with other women. It may be sports (spectator or participant), work, a hobby, a club, a philosophy – whatever is irrelevant to sex and romance. In fact, with so many women working with men on equal ground and showing off their social spunk, opposite-sex friendships are shifting from odd to "in," from sexually unsettled to asexually liberated – just like with another guy, only less competitive and more open on a personal level. You can safely swap confidences and learn a lot about how the other half thinks.

The freshness and fascination of this new kind of closeness is exactly why you may have to get clearance with your woman. You get extra love credit for anticipating her concern and telling her in advance how far the friendship goes, and doesn't go, and why. You don't have to badmouth your friend. A woman just wants to know that her man has really thought the issue through and won't get caught with his pants off later.

Above all, don't let your woman feel excluded. Whether she bites or not, invite her into the friendship. Have her meet your Female Friend – if possible, with a male accompaniment. Be attentive to your woman when your F.F. is around. If there's one thing we *all* resent, it's our mate being nicer to friends than to us. Yet we seldom notice when *we* do it to our mate. So be aware, especially in this sensitive scene.

If you want to cultivate a close female friendship, it behooves you to have more than one going. There's safety in numbers here; they dispel that suspicious stench of exclusivity. Besides, they're delightful. One fellow I talked to got his wife so used to him having pretty pals that she didn't even mind him going on camping trips with them. In fact, she didn't notice when he fell into an affair with one. (Ouch! That's the risk.)

Of course, it's no fair going after what you're not willing to give. If you want to fraternize with females, and even if you don't, your woman has the right to befriend men. Really, you guys aren't the libido-crazed beasts you make each other out to be. So relax.

Less Innocent Extras: Your Flirtations

She may be a friend, with a new twist. Or you may barely know her. But there's a female in your social circle who makes you feel too big for your breeches. When you're with her, you sparkle. Your smile is sly. Your stance is strong. Your eyes know where and how to look. Your words sound witty, your tone seductive. She likes your style. She laughs and plays off you. You slip in a compliment. She smiles and looks down, then catches your stare and tells you that you're quite a specimen, too. Your pulse rate soars into the training range.

And when you're not with her, you fantasize. You dream up conditions and a private occasion when you can let go and pursue her. When you say something brilliant and daring and follow up with a forbidden move, she gasps, she's so taken. You've swept her away, etcetera, etcetera, etcetera. (Fade out; this isn't *that* kind of book.) But you know what kind of lady in your life I'm talking about. In technical terms, she's one who reassures you that, whatever its vintage, your equipment is in top working order.

So why can't *your* woman do quite the same anymore? Well, we've talked about time and children. Besides, a flirtation holds newness, the challenge of conquest, a chance to find out that your stuff still struts. You needn't feel guilty or fault your woman. You have a *need* for new blood, a shot in the arm, a pinch in the crotch. And so does your woman every once in a while.

Flirtations can go on for years and never turn into affairs. In fact, they can add enough strokes and spice to life to keep people *out* of affairs.

Still, even if it's *just* a flirtation, you must practice good management techniques. If it's going on at the office or wherever your woman can't see it, you might as well keep a tight lip. And this means not coming home with lots of complimentary commentary and intimate information on Lady Looker. Not to be sneaky, but not to raise needless suspicion either. To calm your conscience, however, you should share your rediscovered charm and vigor with your woman. If *she* benefits, you can get the best from both worlds guilt-free.

Now, if you're flirting where your woman *may* see – like if she's in the same building – figure she *will*. You'd be smartest to tell her before *she* tells *you*. This way, you can avoid a confrontation and the smell of secrecy. But you needn't get heavy and guilty-eyed. Keep it as light as the flirtation. Tell her with a tender tease that Lady Looker's a tempting torte, and she may have a fancy for you. Your woman will actually take pride in your appeal.

But after the jibes subside, seize the time to offer some winking reassurance that even the torte isn't as tantalizing as she is. In effect, do some flirting with *her*. Show her that she can still inspire the sultry spirit in you that others do. Then she won't resent them or you. Even if the scintillation isn't quite the same, sparking up more heat between you and your woman is better than letting it slip away.

It all goes back to the basic bylaws: Do unto your woman as you do unto others. Then you won't catch hell for coveting your neighbor's wife.

Of course, a flirtation may go further, sometimes quite far. So let's venture on.

Beyond Innocence: Your Affairs

If you play with matches, you may start a fire. Little one-night flickers hardly matter. But what if you're in something *really hot*, like blazing passion, and you still want to keep your woman?

So many of you dare to enter into this dilemma, usually more than once, and so few of you use any strategy to get through it. Let's not even talk here about sidestepping snares with your lover. That's worth another book. For now, we'll just focus on how not to wreak havoc with your woman.

Trust me that I pass no harsh judgment on you extra-adventurers. I understand the urge all too well. In fact, I've seen infidelity make people bloom. A few youthful years of fooling around in the dark often fail to reveal the pleasures that compel us. We wind up in loving but limiting commitments before we learn all we should have but couldn't have. We fall into habits too hallowed to break without hurt, yet too hallow to pin our hopes on. And so we seek elsewhere, pursuing a magic that makes itself, a fantasy that lives.

If you want to have it all, or at least more, you can't afford to make mistakes. So take some lessons from the regretted histories of your fellow men:

Lesson 1. Don't EVER risk disease or pregnancy. You may never be able to clean up the emotional and physical mess. Before you more than *kiss* another woman, *ask* her forthright if she's got anything. In addition to being essential, it's smart and perfectly polite. (Believe me, I've been asked.) And whenever you meet her, come prepared yourself to "bag it." Even if she's the obliging party, make sure she is *every* time. These are risks you can't afford to take.

Lesson 2. Don't lose your balance. An affair can make you feel like sixteen again – and make you just as mature. Before you get involved, see it for all it most likely is: a temporary and risky enterprise; a new chance to love and grow; a spring of excitement; a sand trap of guilt; a high that makes you feel alive; a hurt that makes you wish you were dead. It's all liable to balance out, so keep your footing. Don't fall fool to fantasy. Spare yourself guilt and self-accusation later on. And *never* underestimate your commitment to your woman. Even if she doesn't look like the wisest love light at the moment, she gives off a steady, reliable beam that attracts you men like moths.

Lesson 3. Don't draw too many comparisons between your lover and your woman. You'll only wind up dissatisfied at home. It's too easy to forget that they're playing different roles. Your lover's there to stimulate; your woman's there to stabilize. They complement each other, but each on her own turf. If you can sincerely serve and justify two, you'll give them each their separate due.

Lesson 4. Don't deny or withdraw from your woman. It wasn't your intention to begin with, and it's a sign of serious mismanagement. Your woman will sense your defensiveness and attack with righteous tears and anger. Remember, women keep a careful calculus of what's coming to them and what hasn't been. You have to do double duty to cover both fronts – and to *cover up* to her, if that's your strategy. (Keep reading.) And I mean *you have to*. You can't take from Patty to pay Paula. An extra added attraction absorbs energy, time, and money. So you'd better have a surplus to spread around. Not to be preachy – just political.

Lesson 5. Don't take yourself on a guilt-trip. No matter how "exalted" your motives, you look like a fool going on a guilt trip. From all I've seen and heard, more of you men blow a good thing this way than any other. You can blow it with your lover, your woman, or both at once, depending on who you dump your guilt on.

There's the Dump-It-On-Yourself-and-Your-Accomplice version, which is also one side of the Double-Dump-and-Whammy scenario. Here's a man who has set up an affair in blissful self-ignorance and then suddenly freezes and takes flight. He can't go through with it any more. He suddenly can't look his woman in the eye, or he senses she *must* know. (She seldom does unless you advertise.) Or he "just can't do this to her any more" (whatever "this" is if she doesn't know.) The decent deserter at least *tells* his lover that guilt's got him on the run, rather than leave her wondering whether she did something wrong. But no matter how he puts it, he comes off like either a pussy-whipped, Puritan wimp or a spineless stranger in his own strange land.

Then there's the Dump-it-On-Your-Woman alternative, the other side of the Double-Dump. Again a man has an affair going or ready to go when, suddenly, in a milky moment of curdled conscience, he breaks down and blurts out all to his woman. He may even believe that his wet-eyed honesty guarantees his redemption. But it doesn't. He more often winds up having to give up his lover and "do time" with his woman (lose freedoms, punch the clock, and "make it up to her" in all kinds of unpleasant ways). Or worse yet, his woman walks out on him, leaving him too depressed to keep up his affair.

Total loss.

You see, there is no moral strength or salvation in belated guilt. You have to know your own mind to *begin* with. You need some good, guilt-proof justifications to stretch your commitments *beforehand*. And I mean *ethically sound* reasons that you can get and *stay* behind. Like maybe you don't much believe in fidelity, and you express your love in other ways. You don't ask it of your woman. You've explained your thinking, and she understands. Or maybe you have a respectable need that your woman just can't fulfill. So without denying her what she needs, you set out to fill in the blanks. Or perhaps your shortage of earlier experience makes you doubt you know enough about love and sex to do justice to yourself or to her.

What will come back to haunt you are self-indulgent reasons like boredom, lust, revenge, ego, or whatever you try to rationalize after the fact.

Lesson 6. Do decide in advance how you'll manage the Truth with your woman, and stick with it. To tell or not to tell – that is the question. And *if* to tell, *how* to tell. Obviously not as a penitent plea for mercy. Or with any hint of getting even, playing victim, or defending yourself as temporarily insane. And certainly not by leaving around an egg hunt of hints to torture her into asking you.

There's a lot in you men that *wants* to tell – to "come clean," to be absolved, or to bring your woman in on your escapades. It *looks* so *ethical*. But it's really quite *selfish* if you do it for your own satisfaction without regard for *her* feelings. Some women want to know, but *most* women *don't*. You've got to respect what yours prefers. *That's* the stuff of manly honor. And even if told in a strong, sensitive way, some women will react well and others won't.

So how can you tell what your woman's like? Try to find her among the following four types.

1. "She wants to know and will take it well": the confident and independent type; gives you lots of freedom without the third degree; not suspicious but not naïve; liberal social values; takes an optimistic view of men and includes them among her friends; may have fooled around herself (if not on you, some man before) and told him or wanted to; more experimental and matter-of-fact than romantic in bed.

So tell her, but not with sniveling excuses or solicitous solemnity, or she'll think it's awfully serious or you're awfully old-fashioned. Be rational and reassuring. Explain your motives, what you're getting out of it, and how it can't upstage what you have with her. (Think comparatively, remember?) It's a great time to really sing praises to her and your relationship.

Let her know if she's benefitting in some weird way: Maybe you're feeling more passionate these days, or you've learned some new techniques to share, or the pressure's off her to be more this or less that now that you get that need satisfied elsewhere. If she asks about Ms. Illicit, pray go on. But spare all gory details that she doesn't request.

Not that she's going to be *thrilled* for you. But she won't make a scene or threaten to leave you. If she prizes the benefits that both of you are getting – here's a real test of your salesmanship – she may very well let the affair continue. If so, do ask her what she wants to know from now on. Some women only want to hear when it's over, but they'll tolerate it graciously until it is. A few prefer to know all and even participate. I found one who wanted to make it a three-some and another who chose to play Big Sister and advise her man how not to blow it with his lover. It takes all kinds, huh. But there's nothing like a woman staying on top of a man's affair to deflate its illicit thrill.

Whatever she does or doesn't want to know, let her know *constantly* during this time that she's your first lady, numero uno, the best and brightest in your life. Go heavier on the flowers, the lovely cards, the sweet words, the wild passion. To do right by such a rare woman, you've got to do *more* than double duty.

2. "She wants to know but will take it badly": not so confident about her assets or your love, but no loser; plenty confident about her beliefs and outspoken in expressing them; despite frivolities, a hard-nose realist; not very trusting of men as lovers or friends for perfectly rational reasons; probably had a mean or distant father; exacting about obligations and primordially territorial; wants to get to the bottom of things; cares a lot about what other people think; unlikely to cheat on you without giving it away with a suicide attempt.

Not to come down hard on her. She's a little more into power than love, but she's just being self-protective. She's had to survive some mean scenes. And she's a helluva survivor – scorched and schooled by hard knocks. Taking perhaps her last chance on love with you. Caught between needs to merge and to mistrust. She wants to know for the sake of power what she doesn't want to know for love, but she never amasses quite enough of either. Go ahead, she's worth jerking a tear for.

Fair warning: If you cheat on her – whether or not you tell her but especially if she finds out on her own – you're gonna have hell to pay. Fifty-fifty chance she'll keep you, and then exacting a fine and making you repent with prayer and fasting. If you *really* love her and want to keep her lovable, you might be advised not to risk it – for your own sake as well as for hers.

If you decide to play the gambler's hand, you have a not-so-clear moral choice. Do you keep it totally honest and tell her, hurtfully confirm her worst suspicions, and staunchly accept whatever consequences may befall? Or do you keep her in the dark to protect her heart and your ass and handle the guilt of living a lie and letting her live in the clouds?

Frankly, I've usually seen better results with the latter strategy. It's the lesser of two evils for you men who keep your philanderings light, sporadic, and highly *discreet*. But if they could get heavy or become a habit or you value the tell-all "open marriage," you probably *should* tell her, as early in the relationship as possible. Then let the chips fall. After all, she has a right to decide her own love life style and the chances worth taking with you. And maybe, just maybe, you don't love her the way she needs to be loved.

3. "She doesn't want to know and will take it badly": confidently committed to you and confidently believes you are to her; a faithful and devoted girlfriend, wife, or whatever role she takes on; wouldn't *dream* of cheating on *you* (and wouldn't tell you if she did); a contented, careful traditionalist and never the reckless high-roller; more into family than men; likes and befriends those who don't break the rules; strives to keep life running smoothly and on schedule and feels derailed when it's not.

So why derail her? Just to relieve your own guilt? After all she does for *you*? Certainly she deserves less selfishness than that. Or is it because you insist on the "total honesty" ideal? Ah, how noble it may seem, but *she* doesn't insist on it. Chances are she doesn't really subscribe to it herself. She's not the type to share her deepest, darkest fears and follies with you or anyone else. The way she figures, why dig up trouble? Her ideal is more like "mutual cooperation." So why not be noble by respecting it instead of pushing your soul-baring stuff on her?

Besides, if you *did* tell her, she probably wouldn't understand. No matter how eloquently you explained *why* you cheated, she couldn't identify with you. How could she fathom her own impossible? Not that she doesn't know that men cheat, but she doesn't think much of their reasons. Nor would she of yours. But what would really keep her wondering is why in the hell you heaped the bad news on her. Okay, if you're going to cheat, cheat. But don't upset *her* apple cart with it. In her eyes, telling is the *greater* indiscretion. It's a sign of a character weakness in *you*, an act of spite against *her*, or a desire to end the relationship.

Here's where discretion is the much better part of valor.

4. "She doesn't want to know but will take it well": loves beyond pride or power; tolerant to a fault; drives an easy bargain; expects less in return than she gives and doesn't care who owes who; of course, can be taken advantage of and has been plenty in her past; in fact, may have a life story that reads like a Greek tragedy; sure feels lucky to have you now (so don't blow it!); tends to underestimate her virtue and appeal; has the heart of a saint and the makings of a martyr.

Now, you *can* tell this rare breed of woman and have your sins forgiven without doing penance. She may even let you keep on sinning. But, frankly, it's just one more way that a man can take advantage of her, and she'd just as soon not learn another. She's fragile in a strong sort of way. She needs tender loving ego-building even more than total loving truth-telling. So if you tell her, it'll be okay because almost anything you do is okay with her. But she'll be deeply hurt and won't show you the half of it. However you explain your affair, she'll find reasons to feel that she failed you and to get you off the hook.

Not telling this kind of woman may be harder than telling her. If you're really a decent fellow, you'll feel the guiltiest cheating on her. She's so good inside and so good to you. You'll want to gain her redeeming approval. And it would be *soooo* easy. So easy that it could make *cheating* on her easy. And then you wouldn't really be a decent fellow, would you?

No, with this woman you have only two honorable alternatives; not to cheat or not to tell.

If you found this chapter embarrassing, good – you've learned a lot. If you found it more demoralizing, well – you have a lot to learn. Wake up, young bucks, love wasn't meant to be easy!

Now that you can spot love's common potholes, you can swerve around them or pave them in before they make your love go flat. Now you have no excuse either.

But we only peered into the most *common* potholes. Many of you chose a more challenging, less chartered road: the categorically harder-to-keep lady. Actually, she cuts across a lot of social categories. So even if you think you've mated with Ms. Middle American, it's worth your reading on.

Chapter 11.

Special Cases: Women Who Are Harder to Keep

So you took a road less traveled by; you went for the Adventuresome, the Beautiful, the Liberated, the Older, or the Younger. And that could make all the difference if you don't know the lay of her land.

Special Women require, and deserve, special treatment. They yield special benefits, need special breaks, and make special demands on their man. In short, they cost more to keep – each type in a different currency.

Not that every woman isn't "special" in some way. Even Minnie Mousy offers a unique blend of virtues to the hearth-and-home-minded fellow. But she comes – well, let's say – less expensive. A few kids, an affordable mortgage, and a monastic tolerance for dullness puts you in like Flynn. Not so with the higher risk, often higher interest stocks I'm giving tips on.

So who's "special," and what are their carrying charges? Most men learn only by especially painful experience. But you don't have to. You can learn here and now and how to keep her.

The Adventurous Woman

No need to say a lot here. We already met up with her in Chapters 4 and 10. And if you're in love with one, you'll recognize her immediately. She may be most men's Mixed Blessing, but if she's *your* godsend, be advised: Give her plenty of freedom! If you don't, she'll just take it (and eventually her leave as well). If you *do*, she'll love you more than the parachute ride over Puerto Vallarta. And whatever new scent she happens to track, she'll find her way home to you wagging her tail.

This type of breed *needs* the room to explore life, with or without you, no less than air and water. It's her self-expression, her philosophy, with no slight to her man intended. Like the legendary Ramblin' Man or Easy Rider, the kind of buck who can't be broken till he's thirty or so. Only that's the age *her* adventure itch really kicks in.

So try to identify. Try to participate. Enjoy yourself and her unquenchable zest. But the bottommost line is *trust her*. Trust her exuberant judgment; it's not as impetuous as it looks. Trust her devotion to you, even if she doesn't express it by following your lead or doing your laundry or promising you carnal fidelity. You'll reap rewards in energy and respect.

The Liberated Woman

Just to be involved with this woman, you must be halfway liberated yourself, and proud of it. Trouble is, *halfway* isn't good enough with her. Or so you're learning.

We all *believe* in some brand of liberation. But a Liberated Woman insists in *living* what she believes, and what you profess to. She's got an ideology that goes from innocent generalizations, like "equal rights" to sensitive specifics, like "I cook, so you clean." She can be annoyingly exacting about what's politically correct in love. It's not that she's selfish or hates men (at least not in theory and *certainly* not you). But she can come off that way if you don't understand her.

So how do you handle this man-challenging woman? No, not by becoming a pussy. Or trying to act more-dominant-than-thou. Try this instead:

Ask her to discuss her brand of liberation with you. Believe me, there're as many different brands of liberation as there are women. You'll score trust points just for asking – more if you show empathy and interest. And besides, you *need* this information. It affects *your* life style, too. If you've got disagreements, tell her. But be cool; this is one place to play the "unemotional male." Negotiate. Compromise. Or agree to part ways. Just don't save up hassles for when the dishes pile up or she flips you over in bed.

If her brand bends her to anger, never feed hers with yours. Choose *any* other time to bite or blow *except* when *she* is. Figure that she's coming from a reservoir of anger. So just let her drain it off. Don't add to the reserve. You might subtly remind her that her anger isn't all about *you*, and advise her how she can aim the run-off at the more deserving causes.

Allow, encourage, even applaud her independence. And she'll feel no need to demand more or prove it to you. Praise her lavishly on her career and civic successes. Suggest she take that auto mechanics course. Send her off with a smile on her women's night out, and she won't say a bad word about you.

When it comes to household chores and expenses, treat her like a male roommate (albeit, one neater than your last one). Pull your fair half of the load. In fact, if you come along willingly, you may even be rewarded with having to do less.

Count your blessings. And get her to help you. Liberated living has its benefits for you gents. You can hold your head high and be expressive and gentle. You don't have to know it all or make excuses when you don't. You can cry or get silly, cook and write poetry. You don't have to act tough and ambitious or do all the heavy jobs around the house alone. You can kiss children, smell flowers, and enjoy the wonders of being seduced. In fact, for the first time since Adam, *you can be anything at all!* Except a macho pig, of course.

The Successful Woman

She's not just any old working woman. She's got a Bible-size appointment book in her Gucci briefcase, a closet full of silk tie blouses and Jones of New York suits, a high-level job in some high-powered firm – and precious little time for *you*.

If she's young, she's like the Yuppies of the 1980s, playing for money and status. If she's a little older, she probably overlaps with the Liberated and is doing it for power and self-determination. But whatever her age and drives, the Successful Woman can be the hardest type to live with, if only because there's so little chance to live *with* her. She's rarely home except to sleep and finish work. You're lucky to catch her for lunches and dinners out, and not even these when she's jetting around.

Of course, she's perfect for you Conquer-the-World Careerist men, as long as you don't mind who's raising the kids. She doesn't whine if you're not home for dinner, not going to bed, or not free for the weekend. Hell, *she* isn't either. She understands that you don't always feel like talking, socializing, or playing the Romantic Lead when you've an hour free. You can bet *she* doesn't either.

Trouble is, few of you fellow Careerists stay so committed so long. And lots of you never are. You typically go through a gung-ho stage during your twenties or thirties and emerge feeling that there's more to life than hitting a higher tax bracket. You start to care more about home and family and spending more time with your woman. So unless she burns out a bit herself, you may get to resent her love affair with ambition. The lonely evenings and passionless nights, the gold-plated latchkey around your kids' necks. Playing her shadow at her company parties. Feeling deprived of your Provider role, and the sweet security of holding her survival in your hands. It may be enough to turn you into a sulky hulk and give her good reason to leave.

The problem is really two-fold: keeping her happy while keeping yourself sane. Review the last chapter's section, "Double Careers," and add these to your prescription list:

Don't watch the clock. If she can't clinch a deal because you've imposed a curfew, she'll never forgive herself or you.

Get time with her, not angry. Make dates with her for lunches, dinners, and mini-vacations away from it all. Don't *ask* her *if* she's interested in bedroom frolics. *Make* her that way. Seduce her with charm and champagne. Sit down with her to make domestic decisions. You'll feel better if you help choose your kids' child care. And you'll have fun watching her swoon over wallpaper and rugs. Otherwise, try to free up whatever time she has at home. Either get a maid or be one. And learn how to call up a babysitter.

If you're still feeling like a corporate widower, *tell* her. But *not* like men typically do: by getting sullen or grouchy or stark-raving mad, or by throwing yourself into *your* work so you and your woman won't *ever* cross paths. No, if you want a woman to know or do something, tell her in Womanese. Speak softly about your *feelings*, those tender emotions like "lonely" and "love-starved." They may make you double-over to cop to and choke to put into words. But they *will* get through to your woman, no matter how tough and shrewd she is at the office.

But if you're *still* left longing and you still want to keep her, for love or for money, consider an affair. It may fill in the blanks and get you off the rag.

Liberate yourself. Praise her success. Bask in it. Brag about it. She'll love your plaudits. Everyone will think that you've got a great thing going and that you're man enough to feel secure enjoying.

The times have been a-changin'. You no longer have to bring home the bigger slab of bacon to keep your pride with your woman. Besides, her success is *never* your failure. In fact, it reflects well on your male ego, your taste in ladies, and your woman-holding appeal. After all, it's obvious she's not sticking around for your money. No, your only possible failure is starting to *think* you're a failure. And what really turns off a Successful Woman isn't a man who drags in less but one who drags *himself down*. She may even decide to split to "save" him. And I talked to a couple of women who did.

Believe it or not – and I swear it's true – the two men I know who best handled their woman's shot to the top got out of the competition entirely. One went back to school for a decade and earned just some fun money on the side. The other became a full-time househusband, happier than any housewife I've met. He built and maintains a beautiful home, is raising two beautiful children, and pursues every interest and hobby he wants. When his wife ends her thirteen-hour workday, he refreshes her with his fine cuisine and well planned evening entertainment, often just a great conversation. Since he saves them so much money in services that working couples often have to buy, they can live pretty high on just her paycheck.

No, these wives don't mind the role reversal, and there's nothing weird about them. If your Successful Woman shares their view, why not make a second career out of keeping her happy?

The Materialistic Woman

She shares with the Successful Woman a strong drive to make it, only she demands that *you* make it for *her*. When she found you, she assumed you would. You were, or were almost, a doctor, a lawyer, or a corporate chief. So she might not have laid out all of her terms on the table, but they weren't for richer or for poorer. They were only for richer.

She doesn't agree with Mother's advice, "It's as easy to love a rich man as a poor man." She couldn't possibly love a poor man. And if for any reason you become poor, or less rich, she may discard you like last year's wardrobe.

In case your status hasn't slipped and you're not yet sure if you have this type of woman, allow me to sketch you a profile. She probably hails from the upper-middle class or higher. She doesn't work and doesn't want to, or she has a career that just about covers her clothing, dry-cleaning, and cosmetic bills. No drug elevates her mood as high as does getting "new things": the newest fashions, newest cars, new jewelry, new houses (preferably more than one). Which explains why she's always out shopping.

Not to portray her as not worth keeping. She usually looks like a Jaguar, and she keeps herself up like a classic. She entertains like Martha Stewart, runs the home like a CEO (takes the big bonuses, too), and may even manage the household finances. She'll lie for you, do her best by the kids, and may have a Blue Chip IQ. Besides all the services she provides or subcontracts, she basically leaves you alone. She demands little time, little talk, and little lovin'. As long as you're off making money, of course.

So how do you keep her? She's easy. Just keep the big bucks flowin' in – bigger each year to keep her really happy. And let her spend *all* she wants *how* she wants, without having to hear your bourgeois objections. Then every so often surprise her with some little token of your affluence – perhaps a little diamond or a little Mercedes or little trip around the world. Nothing more. No heavy psychology. But, God help you, nothing *less*.

The Beautiful Woman

She's the undisputable 9 or 10, not just to you but to anyone with eyes. She turns heads in restaurants. They figure she must be a movie star with a face so symmetric, so smooth, so perfect. No cute little flaws, no interesting twists, no feature too this or too that. Just simple, classically sculptured lines between chiseled cheeks and resplendent rich hair. Whether a brunette American Beauty Rose, a russet-rimmed Venus, or a golden-crowned Queen, she makes everyone else green with envy. Including of *you*, you lucky dude!

But chances are you didn't get her by luck. You *set out* to find Beauty and cut a *bargain* to get it. You offered her money, career breaks, or a Cary Grant image to complement hers. And you're willing to tolerate the worst in her, which frankly can get pretty bad.

You see, Beautiful Women *know* they are. And they know men will cut costly deals to have them. So they may hold out for more than will other gals. In fact, among men who have or have had them, these women are suspect for taking advantage of a man. A few of you have complained: "She never lets me know where I stand with her." "She throws tantrums to get her way." "She just sits there all day and looks pretty." "All the men buzz around her, and she leads them on. It gets me insanely jealous!"

Yes, indeed, she can be quite a challenge! She's often materialistic to boot. In fact, quite a few men burn out on their Beauty and have better luck with 7's and 8's.

Some contend that Beautiful Women have it *tough* because all the fellows are scared to ask them out and get shot down. Well, it's true that, for whatever reasons, they don't have many dates with guys their own age. But they're mobbed by *older* dudes – sometimes *real* old, *real rich* dudes, who treat them like Helen of Troy. (I'd love to name off some well-know gents who went after the Beauties I've known, but there are libel laws.)

Not to take anything away from her, but you must understand her unusual background and how it's affected her. She has escaped many standard problems in life, and this makes her *different* – purer in ways, simpler, surer, less wrinkled by life. She has always possessed a powerful resource. And now *you're* enjoying it, too. She's your crowning accomplishment, on top of your others. And doesn't she make you proud! To everyone who sees her – and every eyeball finds her – she says something special about *you*. You got yourself a Beauty and all the rights, honors and privileges thereof.

So if you want to keep her, and keep her tame....

Get hip to the market. Accept the fact that she's got a higher market value, as mating and meet markets go. You can bet she knows it, too. So according to the rules, you pay a higher price. She may feel it fair to be more demanding or to be less loving than you'd like. Just be hip to what's getting transacted.

Unless you push her to go to seed – and she's more likely to go good-bye – you've just got to learn to put up with it. Of course, it would be great to discuss the exchange and ask her for mercy, but power dies hard.

Play to her "attention type." If she *wants* more attention, she's been *telling* you – with nags and jabs, bitches and tears, or leers at other men. You'd better respond and pay fair market price. But Beautiful Women more often want *space*. They're used to being *too* attended to. So they brush off anyone who even *vaguely* fawns. So why keep coming back for more heartfelt abuse? It's better to leave her alone when she's distant. Just keep out your welcome mat, and wait for the thaw. Which reminds me….

Be cool. Beautiful Women act poised, self-assured. Confidence seems to gleam from their smile. In fact, it looks weird when one of them loses it – freakish like "Carrie" or tragic like Marilyn. Not that they don't have their sensitive spots, but they're not so easy to find.

So she wants *you* to act the *same* way. We all want others to act the way we do, at least in the ways that we like. And she *likes* her act; she does it *well*. So you've got to don confidence, even *cockiness* for her. If your heart's sinking about something, tell her. But go down with dignity.

This means when other men pay her homage, and she basks in the pagan procession, *don't protest*. Bask in it *with her*. It's as much a slap on *your* back as hers. And it's part of the luxury tax levied on Beauty. Everyone wants it. Just enjoy being rich. She'll get her strokes. The captivated guys will get a rise. And you'll keep your Beautiful Woman.

The Younger Woman

A hot stock. If she's beautiful, too, a speculator's scoop. What you men won't give for smooth skin and a girlish giggle! Especially when you're at the age that makes them feel illicit. And they are illicit, or you wouldn't raise eyebrows. You must have left some older gal pining in pieces at home. Yes, having a nymph is naughty and nice. Like keeping a mistress American-style.

It's hard to hold on to a younger woman, aside from the fact that, like money, you can't take her with you. She likes older men because they're settled and established, and they know who they are. They're past their lean and angry years. They are gentlemen to their ladies. If you fit the profile, you've got a good start. But there's more to be mindful of.

Stay as young as you felt when you first fell in love. Remember how she made you feel – like forty-five going on thirty. So if you're fifty or sixty now and *feeling* it, you just aged twenty or thirty years on her. And frankly, sir, you can't afford to. The man she loves is *young at heart*.

So how do you stay that way? Start with your body. Keep it trim and fit. Then deck it out with a young dude's flair – show a little chest, splash a little color, try Preppie Oxfords and argyles. Enlist your young lady as your fashion consultant.

Then move on to your mind. Cultivate a youthful crowd, starting with your woman's friends. As Mama said, you're the company you keep. Plug yourself into the youth culture, starting with electronics and social networks. Check out the younger generation's music, fashions, visions, values, and dreams. You don't have to *love* them. Just try seeing the world through youthful eyes, and you can throw your bifocals away.

Get it up often. A nymph can be a maniac. No putting yourself out to pasture now. The years may have slowed you down a bit. But as any savvy sage will tell you, sex is (almost) all in your mind. When you find your energy dropping, it's usually because you've set your mind on other things, and sex has simply slipped it. This happens to a lot of thirtyish and fortyish men when they turn to courting a career. Then they blame their plummeting passion on male physiology. Cock fop! Anyone who has ever had a midlife affair will attest that they found limitless reserves of libido.

If you need to tap into yours, all you've got to do is set your mind to it. Go prospecting for peekaboo pictures and apparel, and dig up fantasies that turn you on. Then think about them as often as you can. A little mental sexercise on your way home from work should help get you up for the evening.

Be her partner, not her pop. If your cherub was fresh out of childhood when you found her, chances are she *wanted* some fathering. She looked to you to mold her mind, to wise her up to the ways of the world.

But as maiden matures, watch out. She may acquire a militantly independent mind of her own. It attacks at anything that moves to put her down. So all of a sudden, she pooh-poohs your advice and blasts you for acting patronizing. You're told you don't treat her like an equal, that you don't take her seriously enough. This can be a real crisis for a cross-generational couple. And if you don't give up your guru gig, you may have to give up your woman.

So let her *grow*, or let her *go*. Better yet, do some growing with her. Get a feel for the forces that make her think differently. *Listen* to her when she lays out her reasons. Probe without preaching. Show her respect. Then give her the chance to even the score and influence *you* for a change. Try on her values for size. Be tolerant where they feel a little loose or too tight. If age has made you wiser, you know you don't know it all.

If you can't stop playing Father Knows Best, Mister, you got a problem. Either you picked up with a certified flake – and what might that say about *you*? – or you've got a Napoleonic need to domineer. If you don't think that's a problem, just keep track of the number of ingénues you go through. Watch them turn into women and walk away.

The Older Woman

It's about time society is coming around to accepting this sexually impeccable pairing – the lustful young gent and the fully ripened woman, yours for the picking. And *you* were one of the unhung-up dudes to get in the best of the harvest! It doesn't feel like getting robbed from the cradle, does it? And she doesn't behave like your mother, does she? No, far be it from *her* to discipline you. If anything, she's a bit naughtier!

For certain, no woman could appreciate you more than an older one. No woman will say "no" less often. She loves your lean skin so snug around your muscles, your high-slung derriere, your taut tummy, your lithesome pelvis and loin. She's been used to a less scenic lay of the land.

Not that you're *only* a sight for sore eyes. She probably sees great potential in you. But rather than glide with it, she wants to *guide* it. And who could be better at taking you places that you've never been before?

To be unromantically frank, demographics help draw you together. There's a shortage of males past the twenties, and it's really severe from the forties on up. That leaves a big surplus of seasoned women playing musical chairs for mates. You younger prospects are in better supply and more likely to lie unclaimed.

But don't think that your madam's so desperate that she'll settle for nails, snails, and puppy dog tails just for a plot of man. She's developed her *own* life turf over the years and can manage just fine without your help, thank you. So you have to agree to a few special terms. Anxious young rams who try to buck them lose.

Don't try to remold her. An older woman has been around. She's even been on her own at times. Along the way, she's learned a lot – who she is, what works for her, what's worth believing in and what isn't. She's probably acquired tolerance, too. But she's not about to adopt someone else's world view. Not even the one of the man she loves.

She grew up in a somewhat different time and place from yours. For example, she may be as sweet as can be. But if she went through the sixties with the Civil Rights Movement, the Vietnam War, and all manner of life-style experiments, don't be too surprised to find a rock-throwing radical streak inside her. Or the marital mores of a rabbit colony.

Discuss all you want, but don't argue. Ask her to compromise, but don't try to convert her. You can't, and you'll come off like a cry-baby trying. Just love her for all you *do* share. Don't hate her for what you don't.

This is a tall, tricky order for some of the best of you younger men. You may be the type who holds to sacred ideals, to a confident vision of the life you're creating. All the pieces of the puzzle you've set out to solve are supposed to fit just so. And if part of her doesn't lock right in with you, the whole pretty picture is off. If only you could snip her into shape. Or even change *your* mold to fit hers. But, alas, you can't and you *shouldn't*.

Still, don't think you're compromising your ideals to graciously tolerate hers – at least as long as they don't clash over everyday life decisions. Besides, in case she hasn't already told you, life may be like a jigsaw puzzle, but it always has missing pieces.

Not that you can't teach her new things. But you can't sit her on your knee like a wide-eyed maiden and tell her the facts of life. You *can* grow together, but you're launching your love from different stages of life. She can't go back in time and pace her passages with yours, but she can *think* back and *feel* with you and even help you see where you're at.

Let her do her own thing. This is a lesson worth repeating from Chapter 8. As a woman matures, she gets more independent. She needs more time to herself, more time for her interests, and often more time with her friends. With her kids growing up and her work life more settled, she *finally* has some slack in her day. And it's not going all to *you*.

Now, this may work out just dandy for you if your job, your hobbies, and your nights with the guys soak up a lot of your time. Compared to a younger woman, an older one is less likely to complain. But if you're more a homebody at heart, you may feel like begrudging her time off from you. You may start to envy your buddies who have more dependent damsels.

Or you may trip on a generation gap and disapprove of what she's off doing. Like one young, ambitious Millennial Generation man who needled his Gen-X lady for "wasting her life" on bridge games and bingo. She played her trump card and F-16ed him. There was also the straight doctor-to-be who harangued his middle-age flower child for smoking "that nasty weed" – until one mellow evening, stash in hand, she dropped him like a smoldering roach.

Make her feel young and beautiful. Older woman will leave if pushed, but they need constant reassurance that *you won't*. Not a one of them starts a day without pinching herself to see if she's dreaming you. Not a one fails to wonder why a strapping young buck like you loves a sagging old hag like her (even if she's thirty-five or looks like Sandra Bullock). Few don't worry deep inside that you're missing the feel of more supple skin or the glow of a less furrowed face, and that any day now, you'll run into some rose bud that you can't resist picking over her. No doubt she has friends reinforcing her fears. ("He's only going to wind up leaving you for a younger woman. Almost *all* men do!")

If you want to avoid her sob sessions and jealousy attacks, just give her a good shot of reassurance *every* day. Tell her she looks terrific, that you treasure her wisdom and savvy, that no nymph could offer what she does. Invite her to pal around with your peer group. Let her know that you're proud to be seen with her. And pour on the passion in bed. If your erotic tastes lean toward exotic twists, try 'em out; and don't worry about her getting queasy. If anything can match young manhood for its carnal curiosity and insatiable desire, it's mature womanhood in love.

The Neurotic Woman

You probably think she doesn't belong in this chapter. Like who'd want keep one of *them*? Well, it's different if you've got one. You're sad she's so unhappy. The challenge isn't "keeping her" as much as it is keeping her *sane* – that is, the way you love her.

If shrinks and drugs have tried and failed, that doesn't mean *you* can't do better. *You*'ve got a lot more control. You're at the helm of the world that's getting her down, not some cautiously distant clinician who nods off as she narrates her dreams. And you've got the *power of love* – the stuff her shrink keeps telling her she doesn't know how to find.

Ok, Doc, let's begin with a diagnosis. The classic Neurotic Woman has a negative slant on life. "There is no justice in this world. It's awful what it's coming to." She looks at the universe from the dark side of the moon, seldom ever seeing the light of laughter. "I don't think my fallen soufflé is funny, and I don't think your tire pump solution is cute!" In fact, a million little things will drive her up the wall, so she's hitting the ceiling over something every day. "There was a line at the bank, the dog made a mess, and you forgot milk at the store! What do you mean *why* am I crying!?"

Long ago, she made the mistake of assuming that life should be fair and go like a charm. She pictured a little utopia where things proceed according to plan, so, of course, they always fall short. Nothing is ever quite good enough. Not the house. Not the kids. Not her job. And *certainly* not yours and the salary you're getting. But, you see, beneath her apparent pessimism, she's really a *frustrated optimist*. Life was *supposed to be better*.

It only adds insult to injury – and panic to disappointment – that she feels so powerless to change it. She can't make the kids behave better. She can't make your paycheck bigger. Of course, she *could* change her attitude. But that's *not* where she locates the problem. It's always "out there" in the world and ever beyond her reach. So that's where she dumps her dismay – "out there," especially at *your* doorstep. Whether or not you're to blame, whether or not you can fix it, you're the safest and closest "out there" around.

Now that you've got a clearer grip on her problem (clearer than hers is, for sure), you can help her get a grip on *herself*. My advice is not a sure-fire cure; *she* has to cure *herself*. But you can take the edge off her bellyaches and stock her mind with some medicine.

Beat her to the bitch: Ask her how she's feeling. You needn't have a cosmic sense for when she's about to blow. Just check in with her every day. "Honey, is anything bugging you? You've been upset about X, Y, Z lately. How are you feeling now?"

Don't fear you'll be springing the floodgate. Quite the contrary, you'll be reducing the pressure. She's likely to start bitching *less*. Why? Because you're showing you *care*. You're taking her feelings *seriously,* perhaps for the first time in ages. You're acting like you're on *her* side and not *against* her, like the rest of the world.

She'll find your concern absolutely disarming. You see, a lot of what sets off her tantrums is a frustrated need for attention. It seems to her that *nobody* cares, *nobody* thinks she's worth listening to, *nobody's* on her side. She feels so isolated and insecure. Not even her man tries to understand her – or perhaps her man *least of all*.

So break the cycle that feeds her frustration. Give her a chance to rationally tell you exactly what's getting her down. Then you'll be more open to listen and possibly even *help*. In any case, you'll have more conversations and a lot fewer ugly scenes.

Make life a little easier for her. Once you calm her craving for a compassionate hearing, you'll learn that it's the *little* things – a *lot* of them heaped up daily – that make her succumb to the crazies. You may never *really* understand why they bum her out so badly.

But, remember, she doesn't *expect* life to pull all these little punches, so she's not prepared to roll with them.

So let's say she's got a laundry list. Pick two easy-to-eliminate items and help her eliminate them from her life. If it's lines at the bank that drive her to the brink, offer to handle the bank business for her. If paying the bills makes her suicidal, take over at least part of the task. If it's the kids, tell them Mom needs their love, or consent to do more of their care and feeding. Her job? Help her get to the root of the problem – too much work, too few rewards, a browbeating boss – and advise her about ways to weed it out: how to say no, how to ask for a raise, how to work around a bully, or how to change jobs.

Of course, you know her well enough to *anticipate* what makes her boil over, too. You know she freaks when the gas gauge is low. You know she stews when you're home late from work. A little planning on *your* part could buy you both so much peace that not bothering to plan is sadomasochistic. For you to hold out on these minor issues for the sake of your pride or on principle suggests that you have very little of either. To use them to get even only boomerangs against you. And to think that you can change her by rubbing her nose in them often enough – well, if you don't toilet-train a child that way, don't think it'll work on your woman.

Don't hide the fact you're helping her out. Let your sympathy show and your efforts be known. They'll give her reason to take less out on you.

Turn her to interests that can mellow her mood and build up her confidence. Get her a book on Eastern philosophy, and badger her a bit to tell you what it says. (What it'll say is why she shouldn't let life's little bummers bog her down.) Find her a yoga or meditation course; better yet, take it *with* her. Then there's massage, acupressure, stretching, all manner of physical exercise, and plenty of programs on reducing stress and clearing out mental muck. Getting her into *just one* can do a lot to unfreeze her frown. It could even turn her life around.

She also needs to gain a stronger sense of control of her life, to stop seeing herself as a victim. There are reams of books written on doing this, too, plus a spectrum of seminars and strategies: the martial arts, assertiveness training, self-fulfillment programs, and getting-your-act-together plans, to name a few. If she doesn't have a job, maybe she needs one. Going back to school may do the trick, too.

Your mission – should you choose to accept it – is to *suggest* the options, talk them over with her, show her you care, and *encourage* her. Take a positive approach. Use a honey-coated carrot. Ultimately, it's your only hope.

Whether your woman is "special" or not, what if you *blow* it or already *have*? She's going or gone, and she takes your heart with her. All she leaves are "her reasons," which you can't quite face up to, and a hole in your life you can't fill. God, you miss her!

So you want to get her back.

Well, just in case the worst befalls you – or, more accurately, you miss the warning signs and let it come crashing in – there *may* be a way you can rise from the rubble and put her love and your life back together again. It's probably not what you think, and you can bet it ain't easy. But if you want her back or you fear you could lose her, you'll eagerly read on.

Chapter 12.

How to Get Her Back – Maybe

No use yanking your chain: The odds of your getting her back lie somewhere between those of your making it to the World Poker Championship table and the Cubs winning the World Series. Okay, okay, they're definitely better than the Cubs' chances. They really depend on what you do. The ball is deeply in your court, but maybe it's not out of bounds yet.

Here are nine keep-your-fingers-crossed steps that you can take that may just work the miracle you want. Remember to *do them in order*. Don't go telling her about all the changes you've made before you've made them. She'll be watching you like a hawk for any evidence of these changes, and one slip-up will slam the door to her heart for good.

Step 1. *Don't Chase after Her.*

You'll just chase her further away. The more desperately you want her back, the less you should let her know it. Act like you believe her decision to leave was a good one, at least for her. Your showing her this kind of respect might be just what she was missing from you before.

Step 2. *Find out Exactly Why She Left.*

Ask her. Ask her close friends. Ask her mother or sister if you're on speaking terms with them. Take notes. Be completely open to all you hear. Just take it in. Don't argue or otherwise defend yourself. And don't say you want the information to use it to get her back, or you might not get it. Analyze what you've heard. Talk it over with one or two of your close friends or family members, preferably both a male and a female. They can help you make objective sense out of it.

Step 3. Figure out How You'd Have to Change and Decide If You Want to.

Whatever her reasons for leaving, they usually boil down to *changes* she wanted her man to make that he *didn't* make within a time she still had hope and patience. You may or may not have known what they were at the time, though she no doubt tried to tell you. Or because of the way they sounded through the tears and tirades, you may have dismissed them as "unreasonable" or "impossible." Chances are they weren't, though, and perhaps you can see that more clearly now. Women are the hard-nosed realists of the species, so they rarely ask a frog to turn into a prince or a pitcher into a Babe Ruth at bat.

What you've got to decide is if *you want* to make the changes *she wants*. Look over the list. Do you want to be the kind of man she's asking for? Are you willing to put in the effort honestly and enthusiastically? If not, give up the ghost. You may thoughtfully decide she's just not worth that much to you, and that's okay. Now you're free to go off and find some woman who'll love you just the way you are or how *you want* to be.

If, on the other hand, you decide that you *do* want to become pretty much what she wants, and you're willing to do what it takes, read on.

Step 4. Make Some Changes.

Before you even tell her what you're doing, and while you have the motivation, tackle first those changes you can get quick results on. Lose some weight and start getting into shape. Clean up the house and *keep* it that way. Read some books on interpersonal communication and try out some techniques on a close friend or family member. Get into the habit of working 10 instead of 14 hours a day. Start *thinking* more about sex and *practice* getting turned on. Whatever you can start with from your list. Seeing quick results on the easier-to-make changes will keep you inspired to take on the tough ones.

Step 5. Get Help.

Don't expect to go it all alone. Maybe you can't, and you shouldn't have to. This is not time for rugged individualism. For a lot of changes, you won't even be able to measure your progress without your woman around. And you might fool yourself into thinking that your recent change of heart and resolve is all it takes. It's not.

You ought to seek professional help on some matters. Start with a licensed marriage and family counselor. This type of help is tailor made to current needs, cheaper than most other sources, and usually partially covered by your health insurance. Or if you're so inclined, see your pastor or rabbi; he or she is trained in this kind of work, too.

Of course, only *you* can determine your need for help. But you can be certain you do if your problem is alcohol, drug abuse, wife-battering (to *any* degree), temper, paternalism, possessiveness, impotency, a fear of intimacy, severe difficulties communicating, or an inability to make or follow through on commitments.

You can get referrals from close friends and family. You'll be surprised at the number of people you know who have sought help themselves. Don't be afraid of counselors; they've heard it all hundreds of times before and can't be fazed. If you don't like the one you start with, switch. They're *not* all alike.

Step 6. Now, Tell Her What You've Been Doing.

Now you have some results to show her, or at least evidence of your good faith and resolve. Getting counseling especially will soften her heart.

You don't have to prostrate yourself with an "I was wrong" routine. If she's worth winning back, she doesn't want to hear that or rub your nose in it. Your approach should be manly and gallant. Tell her, "I'm stronger now. I'm feeling better about myself." After all, aren't you? She'll be encouraged to feel better about you, too.

But don't ask her to come back to you *yet*. Tell her what you've accomplished so far and what your goals and timetables are, and just ask her to *think* about it. Avoid heavy-handedness and sweet talk. Approach her differently than you ever have in the past. Stick with a very soft-sell strategy. Remember, she doesn't trust you anymore. Buyer beware is her byword now. And *don't push it*. Don't pester her with too many visits, calls, and letters. Just give her facts about "the new you" and lots of room to reconsider.

Step 7. Invite Her to Help.

You're *still* not asking her *back* exactly. You're inviting her to *see* you somewhat regularly – maybe to practice some new communication methods, or to teach you her housekeeping wizardry, or to discuss what a woman (that is, *she*) wants in an intimate relationship. You'll also want to invite her to participate with you to some degree in your counseling, assuming you're getting it and your counselor approves. In other words, try to subtly transform your individual counseling into relationship counseling. She could stand a little help herself, right? This is a great way to get her through the office door without her having to admit her own shortcomings.

This step is a real acid test of her openness to reconciling. If she says "no" after two invitations, you're probably out of luck with her. Rest assured that you've done all you could in good faith. If that's not sufficient consolation, think self-appreciatively of all the good changes you've made in yourself. They're money in the bank. You'll be cashing them in on a richer relationship next time with a finer woman than you could have gotten otherwise.

If your (ex-)woman takes you up on your invitation, you're halfway home to her heart. But remember, that's only *halfway* home. You can't afford any false sense of security now. *Follow through*. Keep up your progress. Watch how the counseling is going. Don't rush a resolution. If things are progressing nicely over even a rocky road, read on.

Step 8. NOW, Ask Her Back.

I know it's been a long haul for you. You've been dying to get to this stage. But now at least, your chances of getting her back are quite good. In fact, by now, she may have already asked you to take *her* back.

Asking a woman back is a lot like asking her to marry or live with you: You don't do it until you're pretty sure she'll say yes.

Getting a "no" is too degrading an experience to risk. In addition, it helps your chances to romanticize the occasion. Pick a special place to do it. Accompany your asking with a lovely enduring gift, like jewelry (but keep the receipt). Do it with style and class. You know you'll need all the help you can get.

If she still gives you a "no" at this point, don't let her run off without finding out why. If you can, do it in the counselor's office where the ground rules are clear and clean. You'll get some very valuable information about both her and yourself.

Step 9. Stay the Man You've Become.

No, it's not all over yet. If you *did* get her back, you've got to *keep* her back. After a woman has left a man *once*, she knows that she can do it and survive. She's learned how she can cope with the experience, so it's a lot easier for her to do it *again* than it was the first time. And since you've raised her expectations of you, she'll be more easily disappointed if you slip.

This means that you have to *stay* on your toes. But now you've got more help than you did when you first started your changes. Now you've got *her*, a more positive view of yourself, and a lot more psychological resources than you did before. If you still get discouraged occasionally, check out Chapter 14, "Is it Worth the Effort?" for a dosage of inspiration.

Chapter 13.

When to Let Go

Whether your noblest attempt to get her back didn't work out so well, or you're wondering if it's worth trying; or even if she's still around but the warning signs tell you your number's up, you need to know when to fold. And just as you do in a poker game, figure a woman's not bluffing.

You men are much sharper at cards than at love, though. You tend to hang on to your woman; your hope springs eternal long after it's lost. So you dump all your chips on a losing hand. Same when you're trying to *change* her, too. So allow me to save you some time at the tables. Cut your losses and *let her go* when she deals you deuces like these:

She Insists You Make Changes You Don't Want to Make.

Maybe you're in the middle of trying to get her back. Or maybe she's saying she'll leave you if you don't follow the law she's been laying down. So what does she want you to do? And *should* you? If it's anything vaguely reasonable, or something you *know* deep inside your glands that would make you a better man, *then do it* – or be left for dead. You'll jerk no tears out of her or me.

Sure, compromise. Yes, shrewdly negotiate. Get something out of her in return. *But heed her word.* Don't sulk or stalk out, and don't accuse her of "making demands." Some are perfectly fair. If you don't shape up for your woman now, you'll hear the same riot act read by the next one.

What's reasonable, healthy, and fair? Here's a list of such "ultimatums" that most women *and decent men* think fit the bill. They don't cost you your pride or your principles, though they may require that you live up to them.

- Be less of a slob. Pick up after yourself and help more with the housework.

How to Keep Your Woman

- Be more of a lover. Slow down, say "I love you," and honor her preferred schedule half the time. If the problem between is severe, like impotency, frigidity, or premature blast-off, get some professional help, preferably from a sex-specialized source. With your good intentions, it can work wonders.
- Be more attractive. Lose a few pounds (she'll learn to cook light), get physical and back into shape, try a new haircut, dress up more at home.
- Be better company. Tell her what's happening, confide in her more, share "play time" and laughter, take her out for fun evenings, take some part in her interests, be nice to her friends. If you're the type to go AWOL for work or for play (see Chapter 8), just do it less often and give her more time.
- Be faithful or be discreet if she wouldn't want to know you have extra-pades. (See Chapter 10 for the ground rules.)
- Be liberal. Give her the freedom to work, play, socialize, and improve and express herself on her own – the same freedoms you take for yourself. There's no threat to you unless you *act* threatened.
- Be together. Control your temper, fight fair and clean (review pages 95-96 for how to do this), and don't *ever* lay a mad hand on her. Work to get rid of those "tragic flaws" I laid out in Chapter 8, like alcoholism, gambling, chronic unemployment, and instability. There's plenty of help out there for you.

Now, these are *fair* demands, the things most folks feel a man *ought* to bend on – for his own good as well as his woman's. So if your lady's pushing for *this* kind of change, it would be a waste not to try to reform. Once she left, more friends-in-the-know would take her side than yours.

There's no need to scare you with scores of examples of men I've known who couldn't hold a good woman because they clung instead to a festering flaw, a foolhardy fear, or nettling habit. You've known them, too, and the great gals they lost.

But let's turn to the changes you should *not* have to make – for any woman *or man*. These are *unfair* demands – maybe okay to request but not to insist on. So if your lady's *cause célèbre* falls along unreasonable lines, feel free to change *if you choose to* and just as free *not to* if you *don't*. Sure, look around some middle ground, but if you can't find it, forget it. It's well worth letting go of your woman to hold on to yourself. So, call foul if she's pressing you to:

- Change your religion, if you've got one you care about or can't get behind hers.
- Change your politics, if she can't debate you into doing it.
- Change your occupation, if you like it better than her reasons for wanting you to dump it. Just don't give it all of your waking hours. Then again, if your livelihood is death-defying or not quite legal, her bitch rests on far fairer grounds.
- Give up a hobby or interest, if you love it and it's legal. *Not* that you shouldn't *cut back* on the time you watch football.
- Drop any family members you care about. Just try to compromise on the time you both spend with them.
- Drop a close friend because he's "different," "crude," or "a bad influence" on you, or because she is a *she* (as long as you're tuned into Chapter 10 on "Other Women: Ex's and Extra's"). Of course, check out your woman's objections. It's different if your pal treats her badly, sports a psychotic streak, feeds a tragic flaw of yours, or is Judas behind your back.
- Change your personality. This is the classic demand of the woman who hooked up with a man to "remake him." If you're by nature the quiet type and she insists you turn into the life of the party. If you've always been easy-going and she nags you to be more aggressive and ambitious. If you love to take risks and go off on safaris and she wants you to work for a utilities company and camp in the Catskills the same time next year, every year. *She* got herself the wrong man.

However, this *doesn't* mean that you shouldn't try to *adjust* to her needs. It's no threat to your identity to *talk* to her more, or to take pride in your work and your play, or to be more expressive, less crude, more mature. (You must know the litany better than I.) As long as she loves the *essential* you, she deserves her idea of the *best* of you.

She Won't Come Back After Best Efforts.

If you followed the steps in Chapter 12 to the *spirit* as well the letter and wound up with wilted flowers, don't beat your head against the wall anymore. By your efforts, you *must* be lovable. Your ex (start thinking of her that way) must have her reasons, good or bad, laid out on the table or under it. Keep reading and you might find them.

She Needs an Independent Life of Her Own.

This happens to a woman sometimes, especially the belatedly liberated. She'd probably been depressed for years but has stoically sobbed her way through, trying hard to accommodate to her cage and taking guilt trips instead of fight. Then again, it's possible that you had been smothering her, nixing her plans and opinions and treating her like a feather-brained child. Remember the folly of "Losing by Intimidation" back in Chapter 8? (And you thought you were winning?) Either way, she suddenly snaps and has *got* to *escape*. She wants out from under *your* shadow and whatever else has been stunting her growth.

To you, her reaction may look like a breakdown or a bad PMS attack. But to *her*, it's her first chance to find herself, and it feels like it could be her *last*. Perhaps she's been living only for and through *others*, perhaps only for and through *you*. She's never pursued what *she* wants, and may not even know at this stage what that is. But she does know that it's not what she's had, and to get it, she's *got* to have *room*.

So why not let her have it? Besides you have no choice. If you can love her from a distance through it all, be a *friend* and check in with her every so often. See how she's doing and help if you can. Maybe her trip isn't against *you* but what you've *stood for* in her life. So show her you stand for something *else* – a bridge from her past to her future, a soft sounding board for new plans.

In time, this strategy *could* get her back. But don't count on it; be prepared to let her go. You might not even want to live with the New Self she discovers. But at least you can keep a friend.

The Hurt Doesn't Heal.

She just can't *trust* you anymore. She can't accept you like before, no matter how she tries. You dashed some sacred ideal or made a fatal mistake. Perhaps it was the affair she found out about. Or the vacation you took alone. Or the last lie she couldn't swallow. Or the umpteenth time you walked out on her. Or got drunk on your ass. Or put your fist to her face. You bent the last straw, and no doubt you were warned. Baby, you find yourself out of time.

She's probably bitter, and not in the mood to grant you redemption or give you probation. Can you blame her? Your track record *stinks*. Her hurt's beyond hope. Her friends are against you and have urged her to leave you for years. It's too late to clean up your act for her. (Just get it spit-clean for your *next* love.)

Now I'm an avid believer in forever-after, and I've watched couples try healing their hemorrhaging hearts. The cure works under certain circumstances: The hurt has been mutual, the score's declared even, and both sides agree to new rules. It happened in one extreme case where he had been *beating* on her and she had been *cheating* on him. They decided they were even up.

More often, a couple's attempt to heal a deeply wounded relationship doesn't take, especially when the hurt is one-sided. The wronged party withdraws or get vengeful, or the love is never the same. So if your woman can't forget the hurt, you'd better forget about her.

You Want Really Different Things Out of Life.

However you got together, you each turned different corners. Maybe she wants a family now, and you want to see the world. Or she wants a high-powered career and you've got the instinct to nest. Or one of you has been "born again," while the other has sped into fast-lane living. Suddenly your dreams and desires conflict, and ne'er the twains shall meet again. Talking it out doesn't get you together. Neither of you feel like switching tracks.

It's true that people can change, but it's equally true that they can't *be changed*. That's why the hard sell seldom works. So don't hope you can change her with a high-pressured pitch. You *know* it just backfires when she lays it on *you*.

Your best plan of action is *non*-action. Stop trying to change one another. Stop hoping she'll make the sacrifice. Stop fretting how miserable *you'd* be if *you* did.

Sometimes it's just a matter of time before one tunes into the other's dream, or you both roam onto new middle ground. A little patience and a soft-sell approach may pay off. But if you don't start moving back together pretty fast, you had best let yourselves go your own separate ways. Life is too short to stop living your dreams, and dreams were meant to be *shared*.

There's Another Man, and It's Serious.

You can, and maybe should, tolerate another man in the wings for a little while. She may need a dose of "new," as do you every once in a while. She may need a second opinion; it can *add* value to yours. She may need the sex or romance, which means that you'd better *shape up*. Or she may need the *love*, in which case, you're in trouble.

And chances are, if she's roaming, you *are*. Bite on this sobering fact: *Love* is the leading case of extramarital affairs among woman – not the leering curiosity that leads *you* astray. *Their* affairs are usually *love* affairs – if not from the start, mighty fast. The old adage still applies: Women tend to link sex with love, the same way they tend to link *both* with *commitment.* (It took you years to learn that in your youth.)

In case you're still wondering *why* this is true, do you remember my telling you many chapters ago that women are choosier than you when it comes to picking a Special Someone to love? Well, they're choosier when it comes to a bed partner, too. In fact, I've heard quite a few swear they *only* bed down with "marriage material." And if one of their lovers falls from such grace, he's banished from their bed. This standard is widely held to, I've found, among unmarried women looking for mates and *married* ones looking for love.

And why are married women looking for love? For the same reasons women *leave* their men. Because, try as they might, theyu can't make themselves love their men enough anymore. Or if they still love them, they don't feel their love returned, at least not in the currency their hearts can exchange. If you're hungry at home, you go out to eat. They may not be *leaving* their man, not *physically* anyway

– not *yet*. But they're on the hunt for a hubby-sub or a full-scale hubby replacement.

Some years ago, when *Playboy* asked its female readers if they thought an affair belied of marital problems, a resounding three-quarters of them said that they did. The men were pretty divided.

Of course, to a woman, there's love and then there's **LOVE**. Remember your Womanese? The first type is inspired by *attention* – a man's making her feel like a damsel desired for her mental and heartfelt as well as her physical assets. It's a powerful love to be sure. She feels *at last* there's a man who *appreciates* her, who sees all she has to offer, or at least things *you*'ve never seen. He makes her feel like a different woman – reborn, re-emerging, reclaiming her personal best.

Still, it's not deadly serious, as though her love for you bit the dust. She's not running off with your rival. Maybe he's just not available. But more likely, he's just not "perfect enough" to *leave you* for. After all, you two have a history together, and Mr. Feel Good is a partial unknown. He'd have to be housebroken, and that can take years. And a few things about him just don't sit too well.

But he's opened her eyes to new vistas on love, and on herself, on men, and probably on sex. No way she'll *ever* be the same. So if what's left between you isn't much, and if you don't quickly make it more, you're bound to lose her. If it's not to some guy, it will be to the hope for the higher-quality love that Feel Good put in her head. Whatever this ne'er-do-well showed her, it sure beat what *you've* been doing.

On the other hand, you've got a good chance to keep her if your relationship still has its strong points – and I mean in *her* opinion – and you're willing to learn from your foe. (If you don't swallow your pride over him while you've got her, you'll just choke later when you lose her.) A shot in the arm from another admirer may be exactly and *all* that she needs. So if she makes her way back home to you, welcome her back; you were *lucky* this time. She may even be a better woman.

So if you really want her, you'll heed the hint: Be a more attentive man! Remember that this ranks among the ten sure-win things you can do to keep your woman. Be *whatever* that SOB was to her – a Don Juan, a guru, an Einstein, a prince (ask her; she'll write you the script). She wouldn't have gone off looking if *you* had been playing the part before. So fill in the blanks before Someone Else does. Next time you luck may run out.

Which brings us around to **_LOVE_** – the higher-priced spread, the Serious Stuff, the rival you *can't* compete with. He not only gives her attention, but he gives her a *dream come true* – a new one she hadn't dreamed with you. He inspires exciting new feelings, too – perhaps feelings she wasn't ready to enjoy when, with all good intentions, she gave her heart to you. He also brings out in her the self she's been blossoming into, which is a main reason you've sensed her slipping away from you for some time. However awful she feels about doing you in, she's damn happy and sure about *Him*.

You may hate this fellow as much as you hurt. (Most of you men believe Brotherhood should override love. But let's face it, *no* brother gives returns like a woman.) Still, you can see his appeal. According to your (erstwhile) woman, he actually *understands* her much better than *you ever* could, she says. He shares her looney love of the opera, ballet, and fuzzy French paintings. He's out there with her saving the whales. His dreams run as wild as hers – finding Nirvana, hiking Kauai, building a Mother Earth homestead, or joyfully wasting away in the suburbs.

You can call him a Con Man, a Nut, or a Wimp. (You men can be *brutally* nasty to rivals. So much for that Brotherhood stuff.) But your names will never harm him. This guy is your lady's Mr. Right, much bigger than Mr. Feel Good. You can't lick *him* with more romance and attention.

If this is your plight, I feel for you. There's no rougher way to lose a woman. You don't even have the catty consolation of knowing she's as lonely as you are.

But *please* wipe the innocent shock off your face. Even lightning doesn't strike out of nowhere; there's always a storm brewing long before. We're already covered the Warning Signs. You couldn't have missed them *all*.

No, her life with you wasn't bombed and rebuilt with Him in a day. It must have been crumbling *for years* with you, and it took her as long to find Him. She hasn't been happy for ages till now. I venture to say that, if *she* hasn't been, it's likely *you* haven't been either. If you're inclined to debate that, you might not yet know what happiness is.

There's clearly no point in *not* letting go. The trick is to do it without feeling bitter. Maybe you failed her. Okay, don't blame her. Maybe you didn't and maybe she changed. Or maybe you did. This sort of thing happens. No fault, no foul. Not even your rival's. Consider this sagely salve: You don't lose your woman to another man. You lose her to something missing *between you*, something she takes off to find. *He* doesn't happen along until later.

There's Another Woman

It's one thing to vie with another man: Just show you're the sweeter apple. It's another to vie with a *woman*. You can't turn yourself into an orange. So which fruit does your woman prefer? If she's had her share of Jonathans and hankers after the juicier fruit, you might have to toss in your blossom.

Only around 5% of all women consider themselves to be Lesbian, which means that men need not apply. Most get an inkling in early years and don't swear their life to some man. But others seem to lead a happily heterosexual life with a man they love until their kids are raised, then *become* Lesbian in middle age. So, yes, this could happen to you.

But don't be too quick to conclude that it has. Find out her reasons for her Other Woman. Is she just trying on a new fashion for size? Some women try it just to see what it's like. (A few of you men did that, too, long ago when girls at your age didn't *dare* to.) Or they want to be sure if they're straight, so they have to comparison-shop. Then there're a few gals (and guys) who are honestly bi. They may want two, but no less *you*, in which case you're not competing – just *complementing*.

It's hard to blame women for loving each other. Aren't they great? So soft and soothing. And don't they get chummy as friends? "Thick as thieves," I've heard men call them. No secret is too sacred to keep from a sister. They may just be too busy talking, but it's strange they don't wind up in bed more often. Gay men do lots more with each other without even knowing their names! Once again, women are choosier, even among themselves. Lesbians like to fall in love *first* and do up the romance-and-roses routine.

Of course, being left for a woman leaves a bitter taste in your mouth, and understandably so. It means there's a part of your woman

165

you didn't know, a need you couldn't satisfy, a love you couldn't win. And you can't comprehend how or why it all happened.

That's okay. Nobody does. Not a lesbian or gay organization in the world and not a science that makes sexuality its business can explain homosexual preference. Some have pointed to family dynamics, a few to genetics, and others to getting shafted by the opposite sex. One sociological theory claims that if you try it enough, you like it, and you *think* of yourself that way for good. A recent biological one attributes homosexuality to atypical combinations and timing of hormonal releases in the womb.

So don't waste your time wondering why, and don't mope around blaming yourself. It has nothing to do with the hang of your hose. Only the fact that you've got one.

The Perfect Mismatch

Have you ever seen a couple that just doesn't *look right*? One of them is frumpy and plain, and the other is athletic and gorgeous? Or one is as refined as cut crystal, the other is as crude as a cowpoker's corn? One way or another, they strike you as worlds apart, as though they couldn't possibly live the same life style. They wouldn't want to spend time the same way. They shouldn't have ever *met*. Like pink and orange, they clash.

So when was the last time you saw such a pair? Did it happen to be in your mirror? Do you and your woman just mismatch? Would you never wind up together today? Do you have to work to recall how you *did*?

Do you seldom react to the world the same way? When she laughs or cries, do you wonder why? Do the things that turn *her* on leave *you* cold? Do you tend to enjoy different people? Ditto for places, music, food, entertainments, and everything else that's important? In short, do you share very little in common? Is reaching "a real understanding" a chore? Do you do it more with your *head* than your *heart*? Is the laughter you share a little forced, the conversation hard to spark, the love too well re-hearsed?

Do you feel a lot less than proud to be with her, or do you suspect she feels that way about you? Do you ever wonder if others wonder what you two could possibly see in each other? Or maybe some friend has already inquired.

When you and your woman are getting along, do you still feel lonely and empty? Do you fear that she just doesn't *know* you? That she misses the best that you've given? And that *you* can't get off on the best that *she* offers? Do you ever ask, "Is this all there is?" and long that you could love more?

If all this is sadly too true for you, believe me, you aren't alone. I met quite a few similar couples, as well as ex-members thereof. They had made their mismatches in various ways: to get out of the house, to spite their folks, to get back at an ex, to have someone to love (no matter who), to "change" themselves (well, that didn't work), or because they confused sex and love. Even some best-of-intentions had bombed. Like the Peace Corps volunteer who wed native, believing love could conquer their cultural gulf. Or the disillusioned debutante who tried to live her politics by giving her love to a ghetto dude.

But there were just as many cases of couples who *started* compatible and later lost their common ground. They move away from their hometown, and one of the bloomed into someone else. Or one of them went on much farther in school. Or, most commonly, she went completely to seed. Less commonly, *he* did and *she* kept on budding. But in every case, *somebody changed*.

So if the alien you've been sharing life with just left you for planets unknown, don't bother tracking her down. You probably don't even miss her all that much. It was almost as lonely as before. (Be honest, not guilty; she may feel the same.) Though she may have left you with dirty laundry, she actually did you a favor: She freed you from a dud of a match to find one that can *really* light your fire. As a friend of mine – a male, by the way – so beautifully put it, you shouldn't *work* at your relationship; your relationship should *work*.

If you're in the process of letting go, you're probably feeling like army mess. At the moment, you're not in the mood to recycle and risk getting shafted again. Besides, you may figure, who would want you? Reduced and abandoned, spirit weakened, heart hardened, and pecker pooped. Women! The very word makes you shudder. They're nothing but hassle and heartache, not worth the toil and trouble, and not to be trusted again, you say.

If you're thinking of swearing them off, bear with me for just *one more* chapter. We'll look at what women are worth to their men.

Chapter 14.

Is It Worth the Effort?

I think back to my old friend Jeff, that pitiful guy I told you about in the Preface, and what it would have been worth to him to have been able to keep his woman, Meg. Aside from his short-term sanity, it cost him his entire academic career. He never did take his qualifying exams. He never studied for them. He never was advanced to candidacy, never wrote a dissertation, never got his Ph.D., and never became a professor. He had everything it took to achieve all these things, *except his woman*. And, oh yes, he got kicked out of the married student housing barracks and had to live in a dumpier apartment that cost three times as much. Last I heard, he'd drifted out west somewhere.

Mark Anthony paid more. After Cleopatra charmed him (dressed as the goddess, Venus – what a ploy!) and captured his heart (as she had Julius Caesar's some years before), they became military and bedroom partners. He moved into her palace in Alexandria, Egypt and few years later, they married. Cleopatra knew what she was doing. Wealthy as she was, she suspected that Rome wanted to invade her empire, and Antony could defend her. Unfortunately, he got a little too frisky in land-grabbing, making the Roman emperor, Octavius, edgy enough to declare war on the happy couple. When Antony's forces started to lose the battle, he got word to Cleopatra's ship to retreat, and then he followed her out to sea. Octavius smacked Antony in his male pride by spreading rumors that Cleopatra had abandoned Antony and that he had followed her because he was lovesick. Meanwhile, Cleopatra hid herself and her treasures in her burial tomb, inciting rumors that she was dead – only she wasn't. Antony got wind of the rumors, believed them, and threw himself on his sword. Alas, he couldn't live without her.

There are millions more sad stories like these of men who paid through the bazooka for loving, then losing a woman. Not that women don't pay with tears and heartache for losing their man. But they rarely pay with their education and careers – in fact, shedding a man can be a real career booster – and they pay with their lives only if they stay with a violent man long enough. This is as good a piece of evidence as any that you men are more in love with love, and probably with the women you love, than women are in love with love and their men. Remember, men write the songs!

Think back to all the benefits you men derive from living with a woman. You eat better – less fat and funny chemicals – and probably more cheaply, too, because you're not always going out for your meals. You do less housework, unless, of course, you live in total squalor on your own. In any case, the woman's touch tends to make a place less of a public health hazard. As a result, you're healthier than your bachelor bro's – sick less often, less prone to traffic accidents, and less vulnerable to mental illness. And as you already know, you live longer.

On the fiscal side of life, you have more spending power. Your woman probably brings in another paycheck and still leaves the big financial decisions – the new car, the new house, home renovations, major appliances, investments – largely to you. You really don't care about the smaller ones anyway. Does the wallpaper border she chooses really concern you? (You definitely care if you're gay, but then why are you reading this book?)

You also enjoy benefits in the bedroom in the form of fairly steady, good quality sex, especially for the money. After all, you don't have to blow over $100 on an evening out to have a "chance." (We won't even talk about what you might spend on a professional.) Nor do you have to dress up, act classier than you feel, watch your language, or think so hard to converse. No, in a good relationship, the sex is easy and comfortable, like your favorite old pair of slippers. You both know your script and what pleases the other. Call it predictable, and it might not be what you hanker for all the time. But it sure is better than nothing any day.

But here's the biggest payoff a woman brings you, one that enhances your mental and physical health as well as your longevity: *intimacy*. Where are you going to get *that* if not from your woman? Sure, you have some "great buddies" you watch football and basketball with, play golf or cards with, talk about cars and sports with, and drink beer with. Sure, they're your bro's. You even have "friends" at work you swap war stories with around the coffee machine. But where do you go to *unload*? When your stomach is churning over your employer's pending reorganization? When some physical condition has you too scared to see your doctor? When you've lost a close family member or friend? When you're seething over the lack of recognition for the great job you've been doing? When you really need a hug? When you're feeling weak, sick, vulnerable, guilty, sad, depressed, or needy for something? You go to your woman, right? There's really nowhere else to go, unless you're still running to your mother.

Intimacy means someone celebrates the good times with you, too. Where do you go to boast about your accomplishments? Yes, you may go to your bro's or your work friends, but you know they'll only take so much of your self-congratulatory egotism. Your woman, on the other hand, will tolerate loads of it and may even build you up higher than you know you deserve. Where do you go when you're feeling silly and goofy? When you want to sing some old Frank Sinatra song? When you want to strip off your clothes and – well, I won't go there, but I know you will. You don't do any of these things in front of your bro's, even when you're all drunk. And if you do them at work, you can kiss that job good-by, huh. But your woman will laugh with you, sing with you, and even strip naked with you (if you play your cards right). Forget about your mother when you want to *really* celebrate something.

You genuinely *need* your woman to enjoy intimacy. At the same time, she *doesn't need* you the same, though she may *prefer* you. Even the most heterosexual women have plenty of intimacy with other women. Remember *Sex and the City*? All the greeting rituals between women – the giggles, hugs, and squeals of delight – are the real thing, fellows. In fact, women often share what's on their minds, especially their problems, with their women friends before they talk to you. That means if you're the problem, you may be the *last* to know. Don't believe the myth that men trust each other more that women do. There is only one reliable reason why two women wouldn't trust each other: They both want the same man, especially if one of them is already married to him. In general, women are less competitive than you are – less testosterone, less war.

Given all that you guys gain by having a woman and keeping her, you lose *so much* when you lose her. It's no wonder men take the loss harder and suffer longer. Specifically, you lose more physically and emotionally than she does, and yes, you may lose money, too, especially if you have to pay alimony (which isn't that common anymore) and/or child support. In a break-up, a woman's major loss is likely to be financial because you'll take your bigger paycheck with you. (Respectful apologies to my sisters bringing home the fatter slab of bacon.) Not to make light of finances, but they don't wound the heart so deeply. Women may have to go to someone for a loan, but men go completely to hell.

Men take the loss harder for other reasons, too. Since women form such close friendships, they can blunt the pain of their recovery with social support. Girlfriends will get together to collectively mourn the loss that one of them is suffering. But when was the last time you cried on your buddies' shoulders at halftime? You're not supposed to show your misery to one another, especially if it's caused by a woman. Isn't that what they mean by "Take it like a man"? It's a stupid rule that sets you up for a long and rocky recovery.

One *more* reason, really the main one, a break-up breaks a man's heart into more pieces than woman's: Usually it's the woman, not the man, who decides whether and when the relationship will end. Put this together with the likelihood that he'll be last in her circle to know – after all, she has had a lot of conversations with her female friends and her family to come to her decision – and she's created quite a nasty surprise for you! You don't see it coming. The shock throws you off a cliff, and it's a long and jagged way down to the bottom.

At first, you think it can't be real, so you go through denial. After that ridiculous stage, you get angry, first at her for being such a cruel bitch to leave you, seemingly out of the blue for no clear reason. Then you turn your anger inward. You torture yourself wondering when and how it happened. What did you do that was *that* wrong? Think back to the behaviors she complained about more than a few times, what you dismissed it as "nagging." Think back to the many times she cried – those awful occasions that you decided either to block from your memory or to flip off as just her manipulative acting – either way, the wrong move. On soul-rending reflection, you realize you had plenty of warning, but you chose not to see it as such and not to heed the signs. To do so would have forced you to respond, to act, to change, and you didn't feel like it. You fooled yourself into thinking you didn't have to – emphasis on "fool."

At this point, you've entered the stage of self-loathing. It usually morphs into its more active drinking buddy, self-destruction.

Pick your poison: Would you like Jeff- or Mark Antony-style? How much of your life would you like to ruin? Your career? Your relationships with friends and family? Your health? Your finances? Your driving record? It's your choice. Or you might want to go for broke and knock them all over. You won't be the first man to do so. But it could take you years to drag yourself out of this quicksand.

Want to avoid burying yourself in your own emotional avalanche of self-annihilation?

Good. First, suck it up and take stock of your own feelings. If you can march into a live-ammo battle, you can do this. Ask yourself, do you love your woman enough to want to keep her – if not forever, for as long as you can project? If so, it's well worth your effort to take the steps below, and they've already been spelled out for you in this book:

1) to watch for the *early* signs that she's going to seed or just plain going so you have sufficient time to intervene (see Chapters 5 and 6);

2) to replace the myths you may buy into about why a woman leaves with the much more realistic reasons (see Chapters 7 and 8);

3) to do whatever you have to do to keep her and to keep her the way you love her (see Chapter 9 and 10);

4) to decide if your woman qualifies as a special case and, if so, to do whatever extra is necessary to please her (see Chapter 11);

5) to try to get her back if she leaves anyway – or, more likely, if you skip steps #1, #3, or #4 above (see Chapter 12); and

6) to give up the ghost when step #5 fails (see Chapter 13).

Step #6 leads to totally different results for you than does letting your woman leave you out of the blue. "Letting go" means that you've done all you could and you *proactively* and *rationally* make the decision to cut your losses, lick your wounds, and move on. The downward spiral of self-demolition starts not with *your* decision to do anything but with your sense of victimhood, stupidity, passivity, and powerlessness. And it rarely ends with moving on until you hit your version of rock bottom.

Is it worth the effort? Think it through like a man. Consider all your woman does to enhance your health, your life style, and your happiness. Then consider your alternative.

www.ingramcontent.com/pod-product-compliance
Lightning Source LLC
Chambersburg PA
CBHW061311110426
42742CB00012BA/2135